Who Car

Effective pastoral care of under-11s in church-based groups

Compiled and with an introduction by Rachel Heathfield

Contents

Foreword

One of the sad things about children in our post-modern society is that they are seen and treated as a commodity, the ultimate fashionable accessory. We feel we have a right to have them but often do not know what to do with them alongside other essential accessories such as career, material prosperity, personal fulfilment... Faced with such competition for space and attention, the needs of children, if not the children themselves, are all too easily disregarded.

The church is not free from such criticism when it comes to the treatment of children. We think we want them – after all, aren't they the church of tomorrow? Certainly, but they are also part of the church of today. As such, our pastoral care of them is of paramount importance, yet we do very little to integrate them into the main life of the church.

When it comes to specific activities for children, churches need to deploy some of their most gifted people and actively support them in the task. This book provides insights into the nature of that support. Parents need every encouragement in the nurture of their children, which is probably the most awesome responsibility that God will ever give them. Again, this book will help us begin to do that.

But children in church are not just the responsibility of children's workers or even their parents. They deserve a welcome and the guardianship of the whole church. The service of infant baptism enjoins the whole congregation to welcome a new baby or child into the family of the church. The real challenge is to go on extending that welcome throughout childhood and into adulthood. That means caring not just through specially geared activities and services (although they have their place), but through special relationships. In our former church in west London, all the children had adult prayer partners, and both child and adult were encouraged to form a real relationship with each other.

I first got to know Katy when she was ten. As well as being the wife of her vicar, I was a governor at her school. She was chosen to read at the carol service, and I was in the congregation. She read well and was congratulated for smiling at everyone. 'I didn't smile at everyone,' she told Ros, her mother, 'I was smiling at Ann Holt.' Some time later her mother expressed anxiety to me that Katy, although appearing confident, felt insecure inside. I told her not to worry, as I felt the same at that age. Ros told Katy what I had said. 'Don't you think I know that, Mum?' she retorted. 'That's why I've chosen her as my role model!'

It is an awesome privilege and responsibility to be Katy's role model and friend, and I do not take it lightly. All of us adults in church and elsewhere are closely watched by our children. We all have the opportunity to become a role model for someone in our church or community. We may not have children of our own, but the pastoral care of the children in our church community is the responsibility of us all. So this book is not a handbook for a few specialists only, but a 'must-read' for all those who may be being watched and picked out as a role model by a trusting child right now.

Ann Holt
CARE for Education

Introduction

Rachel Heathfield

What is pastoral care?

Good question! Each person reading this book will come with a slightly different view of what pastoral care is. But whatever it is, it probably includes something of listening, caring and praying for those in our care. As leaders of children's groups in our churches, we are given this responsibility by their parents and carers. We will find that, while we are helping children to get to know God better and to live for him, we are also building relationships with them and getting to know their needs. And we may even find ourselves wanting to help meet those needs...

Children are whole people, and our work with them in church or related groups needs to reflect that. We cannot just treat them as 'empty vessels' waiting to be filled with the knowledge we want to pour into them. Instead we should aim to meet their needs as whole people: social, emotional, physical, moral and spiritual. We can't meet *all* their needs, but we will care as much for the runny nose and the cut knee as for the tears and the joy, as we aim to help them on the journey of growing in their knowledge and love of God.

Christian pastoral care gives hope to individuals, hope of Christ's love and hope of God as a companion on a journey that at times seems hard. Eugene Peterson in his book *Five Smooth Stones for Pastoral Care* (published by Gracewing) outlines five areas of care:

- prayer directing – the work of guiding and encouraging a prayer life in an individual
- story-making – the ministry of helping an individual see where they fit into God's big story
- pain-sharing – listening and caring when times are hard
- nay-saying – the often hard but necessary ministry of discipline and guidance
- community-building – helping the individual to find their place in the faith community.

It is worth thinking of an individual in the group and working through that list to see how we might be able to provide for them in some or all of those areas. Pastoral care in these terms makes for a bigger ministry than listening to a troubled individual; our whole ministry with children is a pastoral one, including teaching God's word and helping our group to respond to him in worship.

The whole of our pastoral care springs from God's care for individuals, seen throughout the Bible and most clearly in the ministry of Jesus. He has given us a message of hope and new life to pass on from generation to generation.

How does pastoral care happen with children?

Wherever and whenever we meet with children we should be looking out for their needs. Generally, children are smaller and more physically vulnerable than adults, and it is relatively easy to care for the needs we can see and observe. The harder and more complex needs are those we cannot see, those unhelpful ideas children take on board and store in their minds, those untruths they hear about themselves that become a 'script' they live their lives by, the sadness and pain that remain unspoken.

Often these 'silent needs' exhibit in behaviour but sometimes they remain locked within the inner self. As adults with a caring and pastoral role with children, we need to develop our 'antennae' to be sensitive to both physical and unseen needs. It's not a matter of saying 'Hannah's behaving like *this*, therefore she's got *that* problem.' But where children show a change in their behaviour, seeming unusually quiet, boisterous, angry or sad, we need to notice. It is tempting to see such behaviour simply as a problem for us – something just to be coped with so the group session goes well. Pastoral care involves a concern for the causes in the children's lives.

As well as picking up a sense of a problem or issue we need to develop a sensitivity in handling the information we receive; a wisdom in knowing the right action to take.

This can all seem a huge extra burden, if we're in the position where just getting through each group session is a struggle. The reassurance is that it is God's ministry – his work in the children's lives. He knows our strengths and weaknesses and doesn't expect anything that is beyond us. It is very important that we are receiving pastoral care ourselves – that someone is looking out for and praying for us. We may need to take the initiative to make sure there is someone who will do this, formally or informally.

Knowing my group

This checklist is to help you get a feel for how well you know your group members and to think about some of the issues that might be affecting them. If possible, compare notes with another leader or helper.

- What schools do the children in my group attend?
- Which children have brothers and sisters, and which do not?
- Which children have experienced the death of someone significant to them?
- Which children spend part of their time with a parent who lives away from their main home?
- Have any children in the group changed their mood or pattern of behaviour significantly in the last six months?
- Write the names of the children in a circle around the edge of a sheet of paper. Draw lines between their names to show the relationships between them.

===	strong friendship
---	friendship
/\/\/	antagonistic/unfriendly
(no line)	do not relate to each other

You can invent your own symbols as well!

- Look down the contents list on page 1. Are any of those topics particular issues for group members at the moment?
- How much of a typical group session is spent talking about the children's life outside the group: interests, families, school, etc?
- Write down the favourite hobbies or interests of a few group members.

Talking and listening to children

Pastoral care of children depends on the relationships we develop with them as individuals. If the ministry we have with children is pastoral, then both the 'formal', led times of the group and the informal times of social interaction will reflect pastoral care. For example, we might explore together as a group what it means to be loved and accepted by God. Or during a conversation we might hear about some bullying that is happening at school. We might witness a dramatic change of behaviour in a child and through listening to them discover a fear of their parents splitting up, or that the child is finding it difficult to adjust to a new school or house. We might become aware of a family bereavement and know that our care for the child will be crucial as they grieve. But the genuine and loving relationships these scenarios depend upon do not happen instantly. Here are some tips on listening well to children and having an appropriate and genuine relationship with them.

Communication

Level

Remember the children's physical level: try to put yourself at the same level so that you can speak to them face to face.

Language

Talk in language the children understand and be honest. Where there is a particular issue in a child's life, listen to the words they use to speak about it, and use the same ones yourself.

Listening

Listen with your mouth shut and eyes open. Observe physical indications that reinforce or refute the words spoken. Remember things the children tell you, and refer to them when you see the children again.

Context

Life to life

Remember not to talk about something the children know nothing of. Get them to talk about their home and school experience and make reference to it yourself. Remember that children generally cope better with concrete rather than with abstract ideas. Be careful of words and illustrations that may not apply to a particular child – for example talking about family likenesses with children who have been adopted.

Church

In conversation try to tell children of God's love and care for them, whatever the situation. It may sometimes be appropriate to offer to pray with them, but not always; be sensitive.

Relationships

Learn names as quickly as possible. Try to develop relationships with the children that allow them to see your faith in action. Make a point of talking to each child in your group each time you meet them, during or after each session. If you have a very big group, or work on a rota system, decide with other leaders which children you will each look out for.

Commitment

Prayer

Pray for the children in your group regularly.

Other events

Show your commitment to the children by finding time to go to other activities that they are involved in, both church and otherwise.

Attention/concentration

Children are sometimes quite hard to listen to. Be aware of your concentration levels and, if you need to and are able to, remove other distractions from your listening.

Top tips for pastoring children at church

- Be yourself
- Be truthful
- Think about language
- Make eye contact, if possible at eye level
- Relax and be genuine
- Be pastored yourself

Appropriate relationships

In a world of broken relationships we want to make our relationships with children dependable and healthy. Our one-to-one contact with children must be unambiguous, healthy and secure.

1. Confidentiality

We may be in the privileged position of being trusted with a child's confidences. This usually happens only when we have earned their trust and shown them our friendship. However, we need to be careful with the way we handle the issue of confidentiality.

• *Set out the ground rules before you start.* Do not promise to keep a secret *before* you have listened to a child; they may tell you something that needs passing on to someone else for the child's safety and well-being. A child might try and bargain with you that they will tell you something if you promise to keep it secret. Say that secrets are not always good and that if they tell you first, then you can decide together if it remains a secret.

• *Never keep cases of suspected abuse to yourself.* We are bound by law to pass the information on to those in responsibility and potentially to social services and/or the police. It is vital a church has a child protection policy; if you don't have one, get one (see page 32)! Your diocese or church governing body should be able to help you. In cases of abuse, don't just do what you *think* you should do; follow the guidelines.

• *Other leaders sometimes need to know.* There are occasions where it may be important to let other leaders in on the current situation affecting a child (e.g. bereavement, divorce or other major trauma) so that the team works together to care for the child. Remember that the child is a person with their own rights, so seek their permission/approval before you tell others. Beware of pastoral discussions with other leaders turning into gossip sessions. There are occasions when a child may be 'doing the rounds' of leaders for advice or for a shoulder to cry on. In these circumstances leaders need to decide a course of action that is fair and consistent.

2. The listening/counselling divide

As children's leaders we are not counsellors unless specifically trained and authorized by the church. If a child has a serious problem that needs to be dealt with, our role may be to listen and encourage them to the point where they are willing to receive professional help, and then to support them through that. It is not our job to have all the answers.

• *Know when you are out of your depth, and ask for advice.* Be aware of those areas outside your training. Think of yourself as a friendly and reliable signpost.

• *Don't let the child's problem become your own problem.* Maintain a healthy, although compassionate, distance emotionally.

• *If the problem has been an issue in your own life, that does not always qualify you to deal with it now.* Your experience may increase your empathy but try to listen with fresh ears. If it is still an issue for you at the moment, you may not be the best person to listen well.

• *Aim to be a good friend.* You have a split role: maintaining a healthy child/leader relationship and also being a good friend to come alongside, to share pain and joy and sometimes to give some gentle advice.

3. One-to-one work

Leaders should take great care about dealing one-to-one with children. The points below are not suggesting that it is never appropriate to talk one-to-one with children, but rather are aimed at helping us to be wise and mature in our dealings with children.

• In a listening situation, quite deep attachments can be made as a child opens up and makes themself vulnerable to you. Very quickly a child can develop a crush on a leader, with potentially painful consequences. Be aware and beware.

• Time spent with a child alone leaves a leader open to accusations of sexual harassment or even abuse. We must be seen to be absolutely clear of suspicion. *If you need to go into a room alone with a child, tell another leader and always keep yourself in view of another adult. But, if at all possible, try to avoid isolating yourself with an individual.*

• We need to protect other leaders and the church from harmful accusations. If you are uneasy about the actions of a team member, talk to that person about it. If you are still unhappy, talk to a senior team member. Never discuss your concerns with the wider group of leaders or start harmful gossip. Never be so naive as to think it won't happen to you.

How to use this book

This book is written primarily for leaders of children's groups in churches. It could be used in the following ways:

• read it through to get an overview of pastoral issues

• if you meet with other leaders, arrange a regular spot in the meeting and look at one pastoral area each time, using the material in the book

• arrange a leaders' meeting specifically on pastoral issues. Use the checklist 'Knowing your group' to start off with. Then ask maybe two or three leaders to talk about pastoral issues they have experience of, using the book as background. Discuss any general areas in which you as a church could improve your pastoral care of children.

• keep it handy on the shelf for when an issue arises.

No book could cover all the issues in children's lives. We have tried to include areas that are more commonly experienced and of particular significance in the church today. These should also show some general principles which can be applied in other areas.

On each page, you may find:

– examples of things that children might say and advice on how you might respond.

• **Bible help** – part of the Bible which can be helpful to you as you think through the issue and which, in some cases, you may be able to use to help and encourage a child. In some cases there are extra suggestions of useful Bible material. This could also be used to help leaders reflect together.

• **Prayer point** – a suggestion on how to pray for or with a child facing that issue.

For Instance

– an example of someone who has had to face up to this issue. In some cases, names have been changed.

• **Top tips** – advice on how to help practically in a specific area.

• **Further help** – resources which will give you more information about the particular issue.

Teaching sessions

There are five teaching sessions, ready to use with a group of children. Some have separate suggestions for infant- and junior-aged children. These aim to help children to think through and get to grips with God's view of the topic. The themes covered are:

• self-image
• bullying
• death
• friendships
• families

These sessions could be used when a particular need arises, for example, when group members have been asking about that area. Alternatively, they could be used as a series together, or as occasional breaks from your regular programme.

Section 2

About the writers

Sue Collinson has worked as a general nurse since 1989 and as a health visitor since 1995, with most of her experience being in socially deprived areas of England. She has also led youth groups and children's groups.

Jackie Cray is Family and Under Fives Advisor for CPAS. She has training in family therapy, and has been a voluntary helper on a children's ward. She is married to Graham and has two teenage children.

Heather and Peter Dowman have three sons and a daughter. Heather is a school secretary in an inner-city junior school. Peter is CPAS Regional Consultant in the East of England. Both Heather and Peter have been leading Explorer/Pathfinder Ventures for many years.

Buff Forbes is a general practice doctor whose last practice was in a multi-ethnic area of Birmingham. She is currently training for the ordained ministry.

Penny Frank is the youngest of four children, trained as a teacher and has two sons. She is currently Director of the Youth and Children's Division at CPAS.

Ruth Hassall is full-time youth and children's worker at a church in Lancaster. She has been involved in youth and church work since she was a teenager, leading Sunday groups, holiday clubs and Ventures. She is a trained primary teacher.

Jenny Hyatt is director of an editorial services company. She is married with two grown-up stepchildren.

Simon Marshall, formerly a junior school teacher, now works for CPAS where he is the Head of Explorers, Climbers and Scramblers, CPAS's church-based groups for 3-11s. He has two children.

John Naudé is a wheelchair user and a curate in Kettering, Northamptonshire. He is also the chairman of an educational trust called Church Action on Disability.

Jill Pauling is married with three grown-up children. She and her husband are headteachers. Jill's school runs a 'Happy-Sad' club for children who have experienced bereavement.

David and Pauline Pearson, of the Churches' Child Protection Advisory Service, have many years' experience of dealing with issues of abuse, working with social services, and in counselling and training for churches nationwide.

Arani Sen is currently training for the ordained ministry having formerly been a secondary school teacher in Woking.

Linda Stone is married to Pete and has two teenagers. She has worked as a primary teacher for a long time and is currently working as a home and peripatetic tutor.

Geoff Treasure is the CPAS Consultant for the South West of England. Before taking up this appointment he was in education for thirty-one years, the final eleven as head of a Church of England comprehensive school in north London.

Fiona Windsor has been a full-time church worker for more than ten years. Both she and her son have dyslexia. She is currently training to be ordained.

Section 3

Self-image

Ruth Hassall

Each of us has a self-image. We carry around our own personal pictures of ourselves – the sort of people we are, how we look, our strengths and weaknesses. They are largely based on the way we think others perceive us. Sometimes this is positive, sometimes it is negative.

Unfortunately, much of our self-image is based on the world's value system, which tells us that in order to be worthy of love and respect we need to have beauty, intelligence and plenty of money. But God's value system is different. The Bible says that God loves us because he loves us... because he loves us. It's about *who* he is, not *what* we are. That's good news for us, personally and as leaders, and good news for the children in our groups.

We cannot expect to transform the self-image of our group members in the short amount of time we spend with them. However, we can begin to replace the messages coming at them from the world's value system with the messages that God wants them to hear about the way *he* views them. Throughout the Bible the message is told over and over again of how God loves his people, delights in them and cares for them – even more than a mother cares for her newborn child. That is why it is so important to do all we can to rebuild the broken image that children have of themselves. We have to start with sorting out the way in which *we* view and value them – especially those we find least likeable. We need to make sure we don't value children differently according to the way they look, their abilities, their families or anything else. And we need to show that in our relationships with them.

Chat Box

'I don't want to – I'm no good.'

Many children are reluctant to participate in activities where they feel they may not succeed or where they might look silly. Talk to individual children about what they like doing, so you can plan a range of programme activities that play to different children's strengths. Don't assume that all will prefer the type of activity that you like best. Make sure that all experience success in something. Make a point of praising children for things they do: 'I like the little people on your model'; 'That's a good suggestion!'

Chat Box

'Nobody likes me!'

Put them right straight away! Ask the child why they think no one likes them. Depending on their response, counteract it. Tell the child what you like about them and encourage them to build on it. For example: 'I really like it when you help Sam with his colouring – and he does, too.' Often the feeling that nobody likes them is because other friendships have been established and they feel on their own. Perhaps find someone within your group who you could ask to be a special friend to this child.

'Why was I given a fat/thin/short/big/... body?'

It's a fact of life that we come in all different shapes and sizes. God intended it to be that way. Wouldn't it be boring if we were all exactly the same? Thinness doesn't mean happiness. But pressure from others about how we 'should' look can cause a lot of misery, especially to children, so we need to be sensitive in the way we deal with their worries. Children aren't always kind to each other and they enjoy pointing out what they see as others' faults in graphic detail. Our relationships with all the children need to set a culture of acceptance and care for each other, regardless of looks.

'Why didn't God give me curly hair?'

Apparently my sister frequently asked this question when she saw the way my hair was getting increasingly curly! Again with this kind of question we need to emphasize variety and difference, and the amazing creativity that God has shown. If a child is desperately upset about their hairstyle, there is obviously something that can be done about it, but be careful in the advice you offer! (As the years went on it was *me* that was asking why was I given curly hair!)

Bible help

For you are a people holy to the Lord your God. The Lord your God has chosen you out of all the peoples on the face of the earth to be his people, his treasured possession. The Lord did not set his affection on you and choose you because you were more numerous than other peoples... But it was because the Lord loved you...
Deuteronomy 7:6-8

God's love for the Israelites was a deliberate choice. It did not depend on any particular qualities they had, but just on God's loving nature. The self-image they should have had was of being a treasured possession belonging to God. That truth did not change whatever happened.

The modern world sees love as a feeling which responds to something attractive in someone else. God's love for us is a permanent deliberate choice, seen best of all in his sending Jesus to die for us. The more we get to know his love, the more we will see ourselves as his treasured people, and value others in the same way he does.

Or look at:

Romans 12:1-8	Attitudes, self-image and valuing others in the church
Ephesians 3:14-21	A prayer about knowing God's love
Revelation 21:3	What God most wants is to be with us for ever

Prayer point

First, we need to be honest with God about how we view ourselves and ask him to help us see ourselves as he does. We also need to pray about our attitudes to the children we work with. It can help to picture each child in turn and pray for each one to know God's love for them.

For Instance

It was all his fault! It was his fault that his mum and dad divorced. It was his fault that his mum was having to see the doctor about her heart. If he hadn't been such a bad person none of this would ever have happened. Or so James thought. James had reached eight years of age believing that everything about him was bad and so he behaved accordingly.

James is now eleven. Since becoming a Christian, he has started asking God to help him recognize which things in life are his responsibility and which are not. The change in his behaviour and the way he feels about himself is amazing.

Further help

James Dobson, *How to Build Confidence in Your Child*, Hodder & Stoughton.

Mick Butterworth & Nick Inkpen, *Marvellous Me*, Hunt and Thorpe (a book for children about the wonders of our bodies).

Section 4

Gifts and abilities

Ruth Hassall

We all have people that we admire and, perhaps, try to model ourselves on. Children know which of their peers are popular, talented or simply good fun to be with, and they want to be part of their group. They can spend much energy trying to imitate others and yet the only people they can truly be are themselves.

We need to communicate clearly to our group members that God made them as individuals and thinks his creation is good. Each one has a role that only they can play with their unique mix of gifts and abilities. But what about those who don't believe this to be true? We can help them to explore and encourage their gifts in the setting of our groups, and also help them to use their gifts within the wider church.

Some churches have carried out a 'gifts review' for church members including children. Leaders talk to each individual about what they would like to contribute in the group or in the church. A list of some possibilities can help this process, for example welcoming people, praying, getting things ready, music, drama, serving drinks, reading the Bible aloud, helping younger children. It takes some effort to enable the group members to contribute in some of the ways identified, but it is well worth it.

Chat Box

'I wish I was good at drawing.'

'My sister can sing, my brother can play the guitar, but I can't do anything.'

Yes, those gifts are good things. It would be nice to be able to draw or sing or whatever, but God has chosen to give each of us *different* gifts and no one can do everything. Point out the gifts that that child has that maybe others who can draw or sing don't have.

'Why do I always get picked last for games at school?'

Nobody likes to be chosen last for a team, so make sure you avoid this in your group sessions. (For example, number the children so that all the '1's go together, all the '2's, and so on.)

Bible help

If the foot should say, 'Because I am not a hand, I do not belong to the body,' it would not for that reason cease to be part of the body. ... If the whole body were an eye, where would the sense of hearing be? ... But in fact God has arranged the parts in the body, every one of them, just as he wanted them to be.
1 Corinthians 12:15-18

The church *is* a body. We all have a different role to play, without which the body cannot function to its full potential. Our God is a multi-faceted God and he reflects this in his creation. He gives people different gifts and abilities. They are to be used to build up the body of Christ and to reflect him – one person cannot do this alone.

Or look at:

Ephesians 4:11-13 The purpose of God's gifts

Prayer point

If we want to help children grow in using their abilities, we need to spend time thinking about each child and asking God to show us what that child's gifts are.

For Instance

While we were growing up, I so desperately wanted to be like my sister, Jenny. She was creative, could sing and everyone wanted her as their friend. I spent years exhausting myself in the effort to be like her – with little success! It came as such a relief to discover that if God had wanted two Jennys then he would have cloned her! This gave me the freedom to acknowledge my individual gifts and grow into them, as well as having a healthy respect and admiration for who Jenny is.

Further help

Cathie Bartlam, *Two Right Feet*, Scripture Union.

Section 5

Disability

John Naudé

Lots of children have disabilities – 14.2 per cent of the population in the UK has some form of disability, according to the Office for Central Population Survey. The children who are involved in churches are no exception, and neither are those we can expect to encounter through school's work, holiday events and other outward-looking activities. It's vitally important that such children are accepted and welcomed.

Perhaps the main issue for churches is that of *integration:* making sure a disabled child does not feel excluded from the activities, discussion, stories or illustrations that we use. When unsure about any issue relating to disability, don't be afraid to ask the child. If you are aware of difficulties getting in or out of a room, or of problems with other children's attitudes, then ask the child how they would want you to respond.

When thinking of a venue for an activity, consider the lighting (for partially-sighted children), whether it has a loop system or somebody who can communicate in British Sign Language (BSL), and the physical access to the room and toilet facilities. Even if there is no disabled child in your group at the moment it is still important to think through these issues and to be ready to make adaptations when necessary.

It is just as important for disabled children to participate in group discussions and activities as it is for others. Some activities may need to allow extra time for answering questions or for getting from one place to another. Communication may take more effort, to check that a child understands what you have said and that you understand their response. Consider having an extra helper in the group, if this will make it easier.

When playing a game, ask the child which part of the activity they would like to participate in. Don't be afraid about their physical limitations: they are probably more aware than their parents or the professionals of how their disability affects them. There may also be issues of continence management which need to be sorted out with parents.

All children are equal in God's sight. Disability is not a punishment for sin. Nor is it something to pity; a disabled child has something unique to bring to the group by the very fact of their disability, as well as all their other attributes.

Chat Box

'What happened to you? Why are you like that?'

'Can you do this or that?'

'Did God make you like that?'

'I wish I could join in with that.'

'Will I still be able to come on the trip?'

Where a child in the group has a disability, other children may want to ask questions about it, although they may not. It will be easier for them to talk if the leader is comfortable with the issue of disability and is used to treating all children as equally wonderful in God's sight. When asking or answering questions, it's important not to patronize a disabled child by adopting language below their intelligence level. And above all, remember to see the child as the person, not as the disability.

Chat Box

When answering questions on disability, do not use generalizations such as 'We all have a disability', because this fails to recognize that disability is predominantly about discrimination. Be aware, too, that children in any additional minority in your group (whether class, race or school they attend) may feel a compounded sense of discrimination.

Bible help

To keep me from becoming conceited because of these surpassingly great revelations, there was given me a thorn in my flesh ... Three times I pleaded with the Lord to take it away from me. But he said to me, 'My grace is sufficient for you, for my power is made perfect in weakness.' Therefore I will boast all the more gladly about my weaknesses, so that Christ's power may rest on me. ... For when I am weak; then I am strong.
2 Corinthians 12:7-10

We don't know what Paul's 'thorn' was. It may have been a disability or some spiritual, emotional or practical difficulty. But the point is the same: God's strength works in our weakness. Disability is not a result of sin, rather it can bring glory to God when his power is seen at work in someone's life.

We live in a fallen world, which affects every part of our being. God shares with us in the struggles that this brings (which may include disability), but he promises that one day the earth will be made new again and everything that was spoilt by sin will be put right.

Or look at:

Genesis 32:22-32	Jacob's limp – a permanent reminder of his struggle with God, and of being renamed Israel
Mark 10:46-52	Jesus' attitude to a blind man
John 9	Jesus shows that disability is not caused by sin, but that it can bring glory to God

Prayer point

When praying with a child who has a disability try to use the language that they use. If they want prayer for healing, pray for it. But ensure that you encourage the child, emphasizing that they are loved by God for who they are, as they are. If the prayer for healing is not answered then affirm that this is *not* due to their or your own lack of faith.

"For Instance"

I was talking to Marie, a child with a disability, about the fact that she 'did everything in life' just to prove to everybody that she could do as much as they could. While this attitude was to be encouraged, I wondered whether it reflected a wrong picture of how God viewed her. I showed Marie Psalm 139:13-17, and asked her what it meant to her. She thought for a while and then said that she now realized she didn't have to prove anything to anybody; if she was created by God as she was, then that meant she was beautifully made. God loved her for who she was, not for what she could do.

Further help

Penny Frank, *The Questions Children Ask,* CPAS.

Pennie Kidd, *Becky's Pony,* Scripture Union.

David Potter, *Am I Beautiful or What?* Scripture Union.

Church Action on Disability, 50 Scrutton Street, London EC2A 4XQ (Tel: 0171 452 2085).

RADAR, 12 City Forum, 250 City Road, London EC1V 8AF (Tel: 0171 250 3222).

Section 6

Racism

Rachel Heathfield with
Buff Forbes and Arani Sen

The issue of race discrimination is still a real problem in our society. We live in a multi-cultural, multi-ethnic country and yet, unfortunately, some people still won't accept it. Racist attitudes creep in to most areas of our culture, be it employment, education, crime and punishment, or social care. Unfortunately, our churches are not immune either.

Our churches usually reflect the cultural make-up of the locality in which our worship centre is built, although this is not always the case. Within our children's groups we may have children from a number of different cultural groups, or we may not. We may find that all the children in our group mix, regardless of race, or we might be faced with two very distinct friendship groups that also correspond to race. We may need to ask some hard questions about whether the ethnic make-up of our church reflects the church's attitude (whether spoken or not) towards minority groups. However, the make-up of our congregation may simply be a reflection of personal relationships and the practice of other faiths.

Our groups may have a child who is being victimized because of their race. The victimization may be taking place outside the group; but it may also be inflicted within the group. We as leaders need to be aware of racism and do all we can to combat it. Even in an area where we might think racism doesn't exist because most people are from the same race, we need to watch out for racist comments, make sure we have a good balance of races in the visual aids we display and use examples of things from different ethnic origins, such as food, clothes and language.

Chat Box

'Why are some people black and some white?'

Explain that our world is a big place. Some parts have very hot weather. Others are much cooler. On the whole people who come from the cool parts of the world have paler skin than people from the hot parts. But people's skin colour doesn't change when they move from one part of the world to another, to settle down in a new country. So nowadays you'll find people with many different skin colours living together in the same place. And all of them can call that place home, no matter what the colour of their skin may be.

'Why do they act/dress/talk differently from me?'

As you talk about racial issues be aware of your own cultural heritage and background. You may be conditioned in ways you don't even recognize yourself. Explain that when people move to another country, they may retain their own customs and dress. Ask the children to name some types of dress they may have seen or different food they may have tasted. Show pleasure that God has created such a variety of people, and that each one is an individual. Make sure that you always point back to God's love for everyone, regardless of external differences.

Bible help

Here there is no Greek or Jew ... slave or free, but Christ is all, and is in all.
Colossians 3:11

God sees us all as equally valuable in his sight. How we are physically made or where we were born doesn't matter when we love God – Christ is all that matters, and he has been given for us all.

Or look at:

Acts 10	God challenges Peter's prejudices about the Gentiles

Top tips

- Work hard to learn, practise and remember names you don't instantly recognize from your culture
- Use visual aids of people and situations that reflect a variety of ethnic and cultural backgrounds (school textbooks are good for this)
- Ban any name-calling in your group
- Try to break down cliques without breaking friendships – use different 'team' activities with different groupings
- Make sure your examples are not limited to a single ethnic origin or social class. For instance, ensure that your examples aren't always white and middle class.

Further help

Christian resource books on this subject are few and far between but secular youth work and education have quite a lot of information.

Contact your local education authority for help and advice.

Section 7

Achievement

Simon Marshall

Children love to learn, and success or achievement is a big motivation for further learning. Watch a toddler playing and you will see the importance of achievement: the child will repeat an action over and over in the desire to make something happen. When they succeed in squeaking the toy or making a mark on the paper, that drives the child on to try something else.

The American educator John Holt wrote that children do their best learning before the age of five. As a child grows through school, discovery, which was so important for them as a toddler, is given less importance and learning becomes largely knowledge-driven. Achievement often becomes good marks in a test or exam. In these circumstances, motivation can become hard to maintain unless the results are linked to some reward. And, of course, many children do not show their full potential in test conditions.

Motivation can come from other sources: parents can either encourage a child to do their best or add pressure to 'perform'. Parents who take no interest in a child's learning may be a source of demotivation, giving the impression that achievement in learning is unimportant. Children who are compared to their brothers or sisters may feel that their achievement is never valued.

A sense of achievement is also important in a church group. But we want the driving force for learning and growth to be a hunger for God and a desire to follow Jesus rather than just receiving a reward, certificate or prize. All the children need a sense of success, and prizes will give some a feeling of perpetual failure instead. As well as providing activities in which individual children can experience success, group projects can give a really strong sense of joint achievement.

Chat Box

'I'm really worried about my test tomorrow.'

Reassure a child who is worried about a test or exam that they can only do their best. That's all God wants of them. Suggest they ask God to help them to be calm and to think clearly in the test. Assure them that you will be praying for them as they sit the test and, if appropriate, offer to pray with them there and then.

Chat Box

'My dad says that if I work hard this year, I can have a bike.'

Where a parent offers an incentive for achievement, good results or hard work, it's important for the child to know just what is expected of them. If they are not sure, they should ask. For some it may be an unbearable pressure, for others it could be just what they need to get working! Adjust what you say in response accordingly, but never undermine what a parent has done.

'My teacher is really unfair; I try really hard but he never tells me that my work is good.'

Assure the child that this does not mean that they're not doing their best. It may be that the teacher is too busy or forgets to praise the child appropriately. If you feel there is a long-term problem in a child's relationship with their teacher, you might decide to chat to a parent about this. The parent may be able to provide the approval the child needs over their school work.

We want to encourage children to be the best they can be, but we're in the business of creating disciples of Jesus, not perfect people – only God can do that!

Bible help

Therefore I tell you, do not worry about your life, what you will eat or drink; or about your body, what you will wear. Is not life more important than food, and the body more important than clothes? ... For the pagans run after all these things, and your heavenly Father knows that you need them. But seek first his kingdom and his righteousness, and all these things will be given to you as well. Therefore do not worry about tomorrow, for tomorrow will worry about itself. Each day has enough trouble of its own.
Matthew 6:25-34

Jesus tells his disciples to get their priorities right. Everyone else may run after material (or academic or artistic) achievement and security but our priority is God's kingdom: being right with God and doing what he wants. Success is having our will in line with God's.

Or look at:

Psalm 1	Roots in God's word lead to plans prospering
Proverbs 16:3	Commit plans to God

Prayer point

School is a big part of children's lives. Pray for them in that setting and for their friends and teachers. Include this in your prayer during group times, too.

For Instance

Al, a junior school teacher, writes:

'When Michael came into my class he was eight. He loved learning but had difficulties with reading and spelling, so often got frustrated. As I got to know Michael, he brought in books which he had been reading at home with his family. Michael loved to show me these books and talk about his favourite bits, often at the most inconvenient moments! However, as the year went by, Michael's reading improved and he continued to bring things in to share with us. His parents were very grateful to me for my continued interest in Michael's learning and said that it had motivated Michael to keep on trying hard.'

Section 8

'I hate school'

Linda Stone and Rachel Heathfield

When a child hates school, life is pretty miserable. They have to spend so much of their lives there that, if they are unhappy, it can seem unbearable. Pastoral care of a child in this situation means listening carefully to them and asking what is the cause of their feeling. It might be

- a particular teacher or class member
- a specific subject
- a dislike of groups
- school lunches
- being separated from a friend by class reorganization
- bullying
- fear of failure or underachievement.

What counts in our relationship with the child is that we listen carefully, avoid belittling the situation or giving a trite reply, but provide support and hope for their lives.

It might not be possible to make the hatred of school go away. Some of the reasons may be solvable, others will not. We do need to make sure that the aspects of school life which are most difficult for the child are not repeated in the church group.

It is important that school life gets regular mentions in our group sessions, so that children know that all aspects of their lives are of interest to God. General 'news' or chatting times can help, perhaps as a regular feature of the group, as can using examples from school life in learning activities.

Bible help

... God has said, 'Never will I leave you: never will I forsake you.' So we say with confidence, 'The Lord is my helper; I will not be afraid. What can human beings do to me?'
Hebrews 13:5-6

The writer to the Hebrews is reassuring readers about their economic security, but the truth is the same whatever worries we face. To help a child remember the crux of this verse, hold their hand out in front of them. As you say the five words, 'Never will I leave you', point to each finger in turn, starting with the little finger. When you reach the thumb, say their name instead of 'you', and point the thumb at their chest.

Encourage them to try this on their own, especially when life feels overwhelming. God does use our hard times to help us grow in maturity, though that is a tough lesson to learn.

Or look at:

Psalm 20	A prayer for someone in distress
Romans 8:38-39	Nothing can separate us from Christ's love

Prayer point

Pray for the child to know God's presence with them as they face going to school.

For Instance

John enjoyed school when he was younger, but it all changed when he started getting homework. He did not have the skills or self-confidence to concentrate on work at home and so he often failed to complete the task. This led to worries about how the teacher would react and grew into a fear of going to school at all. Every slight ache, pain or cold was exaggerated to avoid having to go. As an adult, looking back, John says: 'Things changed quite suddenly. It's hard to know exactly how it happened. More encouragement from a teacher was certainly part of it. But in the end, I know it was God's work in me. I still see traces of the problems I had then in my life today. But God gives me the strength to face the challenges.'

Section 9

'I find numbers and words difficult'

Fiona Windsor

Many children and adults have difficulty with words and numbers. It may be caused by a specific condition such as dyslexia or it may result from difficulty at school, a reaction to a trauma or a lack of stimulation to read and write. This fact has largely been ignored by churches. So much of what we do together revolves around words, whether it's singing, liturgy, worksheets or sermons. It is vital that we address the issue both for our children's groups and in all-age and adults' activities.

Children who have difficulty in reading are often very good at keeping quiet about the fact. A group leader may go a long time without finding out. Sometimes teachers and parents will also have failed to recognize the problem. And the child may not understand it either. For these children, the frustration can be enormous. Those who finally get the extra help they need after a long time of struggle express enormous relief at being 'discovered'. Where you believe there is a specific problem, talk to the child's parents about it, asking for advice as to how best to help their child.

Some individuals tell distressing tales of how they have been treated by church group leaders, using words such as 'humiliation' and 'frustration'. One boy says that when leaders heard about his problem they assumed he was 'thick'. During story time, he was asked to hold up the pictures as he couldn't read. At Christmas, because learning lines for the nativity play was deemed too difficult, he was offered the choice of playing the triangle or being a sheep.

Top tips

- Use a variety of activities, including some which don't involve reading and writing
- Don't assume everyone can read. Be aware and sensitive.
- Always give choice about reading. Never read verse by verse around the room unless you are absolutely confident that all will enjoy it.
- Encourage group members to enjoy hearing the Bible read aloud. This is how it was written to be communicated. Most of the original recipients could not read.
- Don't make a big issue of those struggling with words; be sensitive to their privacy. Let the individual lead you in what they feel able to do.
- Don't give out long lists of instructions for games or activities. If you need to, create a simple checklist which group members can work through step by step.
- Send information home by letter, not just as a verbal message.
- Do not give someone an 'easy part' in an attempt to help; this is patronizing.
- Identify and include activities which are enjoyed by those group members with reading difficulties.

Further help

Dyslexia Association, 98 London Road, READING, RG1 5AU (Tel: 0118 966 8271).

David Potter, *Am I Beautiful or What?* Scripture Union.

“For Instance”

Paul, aged 14, has dyslexia and goes to a school that gives him special help. For many years he has been going to his Junior Church groups. He describes how tense he would feel at the beginning of every Sunday group 'in case I had to read'. As soon as someone else was chosen he could feel his whole being relax. He has 'no-fixed-reference eye' which means there appear to be no gaps between words. Using scissors accurately is also difficult. He used to get away unnoticed in his group by always pairing up with a good reader or by getting good at listening and remembering. However, memory did not always serve him well. Information about extra group activities was given verbally and he could never remember where or when they were, and so he usually missed them.

Paul warns of the long-term effect his difficulties have had on his church life. The fear of humiliation means he remains unsure of things rather than checking details, so he still misses out on some activities. And he still chooses not to go to some church events in case he will be asked to read aloud.

Section 10

TEACHING SESSION: God made me ME!

Psalm 139:13-18,23-24

Leaders' help

This psalm is a song of immense wonder and praise to God for the mystery of his creation. The psalmist recognizes the awesomeness of God's being. He reflects on the mystery that the almighty Lord knew and cared for him even before his mother knew he was there.

'All the days ordained for me' (verse 16). God has a plan and a purpose for each of our lives. Before we even opened our eyes, he knew the colour of our hair, how tall we would grow, the gifts and abilities we would possess, what we would be like and all we would do.

'How precious to me are your thoughts' (verse 17). The psalmist is amazed that the creator of the world should think of him, not just every now and then, but constantly – day after day after day. The Lord God is personally interested in every detail of our lives – what more of an ego boost do we need!

Aim

That the children will understand that God created us to be unique and that he sees each one of us as valuable.

Way in

Bring along something that you have made yourself – a jumper you have knitted, a pot you have moulded, a cake you have baked. Talk about how you chose what to make – decisions about colour, size, shape, flavour and so on – and then how you went about making it.

Tell it

Place safety mirrors around the room. If possible, also spread round a series of photographs showing a child's growth and development, including one of an antenatal scan. Read the verses very slowly, from a clear, child-friendly translation of the Bible as the children look at the pictures and at their reflections.

Apply it

Ask the children to say which word or phrase from the reading they liked best or found most memorable. Do they have questions about any of them? Talk about their choices and about God's amazing craftsmanship in making us and how completely he knows us. Look at the photographs and the mirror reflections again. Comment on how amazing it is to see how we grow and develop.

Respond to God

Under 7s: Make face masks out of paper plates showing the different children in the group. Encourage them to emphasize the differences – hair, colour of eyes, etc. Then spend time as a group looking at each mask in turn and saying what is unique and special about that person. Invite the children to contribute what they think is good about that particular person, for example: 'You draw really well', or 'You help people'.

Over 7s: Give each child a piece of foil about 20 cm long. Ask them to mould these carefully over their faces so they make an imprint. Put the results on the wall or a table and look at how different they are. Go round the group, asking each child to say something they do well. Repeat this with something they like (wind in their hair, purple things). Comment on how each one is unique.

Invite the children to bring their masks/silhouettes to God as a prayer, thanking him for his creativity and care. For the older children you could include a time of confession when they can tell God about the things they're not happy with and ask for his help to accept or change them.

Section 11

Feelings: Anger

Heather and Peter Dowman

Anger can be experienced in the form of a volcanic eruption, a simmering fume or silent withdrawal. Anger affects everyone around the child feeling it!

There may be a perfectly understandable reason for a particular outbreak of anger, but punching your friend in the eye is not the best way to deal with the problem! Finding out what has caused the anger is often the first step towards defusing and then resolving the situation. So...

- Is it a reaction to unfair behaviour by others?
- Might it be embarrassment (e.g. not being able to read well)?
- Could it be frustration (a missed football shot) or tiredness?
- Is it simply a 'bad mood'?
- Is there an underlying cause which needs to be investigated (an ongoing trauma such as bereavement or another loss)?

For the pastoral care of our group, there are two issues to deal with: dealing with an angry child in the group situation, and helping a child with a temper to learn how to handle their anger.

Top tips

Dealing with an angry child in the group

- Allow space and time for an angry child to 'cool down', then listen carefully.
- Never respond with anger.
- Only restrain a child if they are putting themselves or others in danger of harm.
- When the child is calm, try to get them to identify what made them angry.
- Encourage them to put right what they did while angry (e.g. saying sorry or putting furniture back in place).
- Make sure that you are completely fair in your handling of the situation. If two or more people were involved, hear all sides. If the outburst was caused by provocation, treat the 'provoker' justly.

Top tips

Helping a child handle their anger

- Reassure them that anger is a normal human response. However, make sure they know that sometimes our actions or words while we are angry can do damage to things and hurt people's feelings.
- Is there something or someone who always provokes an angry response? Perhaps avoidance is the best policy.
- Sometimes our anger is justified (when people are wronged or those we love are hurt, for example). Suggest that the child learns to recognize when they are getting angry and to walk away, count to ten, tell a leader or find some other way of keeping cool. Encourage them to talk to someone else about what would be the best way to let the person in the wrong know that they have caused their anger.

Bible help

My dear brothers and sisters take note of this: Everyone should be quick to listen, slow to speak and slow to become angry, for human anger does not bring about the righteous life that God desires.
James 1:19-20

God knows the kind of life he wants us to have: and anger is not part of it. Although there is a rare anger that arises from love, most human anger denies love and spoils the relationship God expects us to have with others. That spoils our relationship with him.

Or look at:

Matthew 5:22	Anger is as serious as murder in God's eyes
Colossians 3:8-15	For God's people, tolerance and forgiveness should replace anger

ANGER

Section 12

Feelings: Love

Heather and Peter Dowman

Take a group of twelve 7-year-olds and ask them what they love – and you will probably get twelve enthusiastic responses! Children have a great capacity for giving and receiving love. A child's ability to love and be loved is shaped by the type of love they have received from parents (or other caring adults), their family and friends.

We all need to be loved and accepted by others, so even children who have been physically or emotionally abused by a parent may well be fiercely loyal ('loving') to that adult. A child who is treated aggressively by a parent may well act aggressively towards his or her peers even though he or she likes them.

Perhaps the only way a busy parent indicates love is by gifts or leaving a chocolate bar out. Or perhaps the only way a child gets attention at home is by being naughty. If so, that may be why they are naughty in your group. Underlying this behaviour is the cry 'Love me' or 'Accept me'. Always be on the listen for this silent plea.

As leaders we should try to be givers of love and thus become role models for the children. We should be creative in the way we show love to our groups through our preparation for the session, through the way we talk and listen to the children, our handling of misbehaviour, marking birthdays, and so on.

Children can become very attached to group leaders. That can be an excellent thing, but with older children there is the danger of a crush developing. While this can feel very flattering for the leader concerned it is not a healthy basis for a relationship and can lead to inappropriate behaviour by the child and/or the leader.

Bible help

A new command I give you: Love one another. As I have loved you, so you must love one another. By this everyone will know that you are my disciples, if you love one another.
John 13:34-35

Love is a key attribute of all Christians – especially love for each other within the church. That includes relationships within the children's groups. The love which Jesus commands us to show is to be of the same self-giving quality as his love. It might seem an unachievably high standard, but the idea is that the unlimited love we have received from him should leak out of us in our relationships with each other. We have his Holy Spirit to make it possible.

Or look at:

1 Corinthians 13	Love matters more than all the other good things in the church
Romans 12:9-21	The nature of sincere Christian love

Top tips

- Show love for the children. Try out the question: 'Is this the best I can do for them?'
- Make sure your love is not conditional – based on their good behaviour or just for those you find easiest. Treat everyone the same.
- Beware of the dangers of a child having a crush on you. If this may be happening, talk to another leader about it.
- Be aware of children who may have crushes on other leaders: does that leader need help handling the situation?
- Children express their love in many ways. If it is by touch, take care that any hugs or holding of hands are done in public, not in private. If it is by gifts or cards, be gracious in your response to them.
- Make sure the children know about God's love for them. Make sure it's a big part of your teaching programme.
- Include in your sessions times for showing a loving response to God in words or actions. Do activities where you, as a group, do something loving for others.

Section 13

Feelings: Envy

Heather and Peter Dowman

The green-eyed monster lurks beneath the surface of most children (and adults!). We are living in a very materialistic world where image and possessions are seen as vitally important – the right trainers, the latest toy craze, the best gear, the coolest haircut.

But it's a very short step from envy to self-destructive anger. A child may be very upset that they are the only one who has not visited Disney World. It won't help if you tell them not to be silly!

Keep an eye open for the child who 'has it all' and who makes sure that everyone knows it! Have a quiet word with them. Boasting is just as bad as envy! It's yet another area where we need to make sure that each member of the group is valued and loved regardless of beauty, brains or background.

We want to encourage children to be content with what they have and be grateful to God for it. Helping children to learn the art of being content with what they have is not easy. They will be much more powerfully influenced by the values of their parents and friends which will not always be Christian ones. But where our attitudes are different, then they will stand out and have an impact. Try to establish a culture of sharing with each other. Learning sessions can also deal specifically with material possessions from time to time.

Across the world there are many millions who don't even have the basics of life, let alone a particular brand of something. Our groups should help to open children's eyes to the wider world. We don't want to emotionally blackmail children, but it can help to remind them gently that some people don't have food, clothes or shelter, or haven't heard about Jesus. That approach can sound rather 'moralizing' unless it is combined with some action and prayer for those who lack these things.

Bible help

... we brought nothing into the world, and we can take nothing out of it. But if we have food and clothing, we will be content with that. Those who want to get rich fall into temptation and a trap and into many foolish and harmful desires that plunge people into ruin and destruction. For the love of money is a root of all kinds of evil.

1 Timothy 6:7-10

The consequences of envy and desire for material gain sound dangerous. So it's not surprising they get a mention in the ten commandments. As a trap, envy is hard to get out of. Even getting the thing which is the source of the envy does not really satisfy. Only learning to be content can give us real peace.

Or look at:

Genesis 37:1-4	Joseph's brothers – how envy can lead to more serious problems
Matthew 20:1-16	God treats all his people in the same way

Top tips

- Don't mistake an inability to share (especially in young children) for envy.
- Try to explore why a child wants something. Sometimes children desire good things as well as not so good!
- If a child is envious because they have basic practical needs, plan with others how you can help with these.
- Support a relief project together.

ENVY

Section 14

Feelings: Hate

Heather and Peter Dowman

Some say that hate is a much stronger emotion than anger – it is a feeling that hurts inside and makes you want to hurt other people. It is a feeling that can be too strong to speak – it makes the body tense and it fills the mind with bad intentions.

A child might be the victim of the lies of others; how can they respond? If a friendship is betrayed, what can they do? The child may well turn to hate the perpetrators in order to try to cope with the deep sense of unfairness they are experiencing. But if they do, they are really becoming a victim for a second time. By letting other people's nastiness get to them, it is as if they are allowing them to 'win'. That can be very hard to explain to a child experiencing such strong emotions, but it can help. Often nastiness is done simply for the reaction.

A child might hate a parent. In an acrimonious divorce, the bitterness of one parent towards the other might cause a reaction of hate in a child. Or in exceptional cases, feelings of hate might be directed towards a perpetrator of abuse. Where you hear clues to a strong underlying hate of this kind in things a child says, you need to be very sensitive and tread carefully. There may be times when it is appropriate to become a mediator or advocate for the child with their parents, but this should be done only after talking with a children's work coordinator or minister. In the case of suspected abuse, you must follow your church's guidelines (see pages 31–32).

A child may need more than an apology from someone who has caused them to experience strong hate. They may need to see the apology demonstrated in changed behaviours and relationships so that the pain can begin to heal.

Bible help

Two other men, both criminals, were also led out with him to be executed. When they came to the place called the Skull, there they crucified him, along with the criminals – one on his right, the other on his left. Jesus said, 'Father, forgive them, for they do not know what they are doing.'
Luke 23:32-34

Jesus' reaction to the deepest of unjust treatment is very far from hate. It is so different from our instinctive response. We can only know that quality of forgiveness through knowing his forgiveness of us and having his Spirit to help us forgive others.

Or look at:

Proverbs 10:12	The consequences of hatred and love
Ephesians 4:26-27	Dealing with anger before it turns into hate
1 John 2:9-10	There is no place for hate amongst God's people.

Top tips

- 'I hate...' may mean a child is just frustrated, or it may reflect a long-term overpowering feeling. Don't overreact or ignore what a child says. Listen carefully to discover the cause.
- Be wise in your subsequent action.
- Where there is just a clash of personalities, encourage each child individually to work at tolerating the other. Explain that there will always be people that we find it hard to be friends with. But Jesus does expect us to 'love our neighbour' even if they are different from us.
- If a child says they hate you, it will probably hurt. Again, don't overreact. If it's more than just a way of saying 'I don't want to do this', then it will be more appropriate for another leader to find out what it is about.

HATE

Section 15

Feelings: Fear

Penny Frank

Fear is a common emotion in both adults and children. Some fears we have as children disappear as we grow older, others don't. Some fear is of the unknown, or perhaps of a difficult task. Some fear is of objects or places and may be rational: like a fear of standing at the edge of a cliff. However, some fear is not rational and will not disappear with logical, detached proof. Some fear is deep-seated and, once installed, will trigger at the slightest opportunity.

When a child says 'I'm afraid of...', the automatic reaction might be 'Don't be silly!' But for that child the fear will feel very real and sometimes overwhelming. Many adults have only been released from childhood fears by professional therapy or by the power of the Holy Spirit.

Chat Box

'I'm scared of...'

Often children will say this simply because they don't know what to expect from a new experience. In that case, giving more information can help. Sometimes encouragement to get on and do the thing, perhaps with a hand held, makes the fear quickly subside. Sometimes a child will be telling you their fear because just saying it can feel exciting. However, this is quite different from fear over which the child has no control. It is important that when a great fear of something known is expressed in vocal or body language, the child has the opportunity to talk.

Try not to ask the child a lot of questions – that will only condense the fear. Use open-ended questions to encourage them to express their feelings: 'So how does that make you feel?' or 'I wonder why you feel like that?' There may be a bad experience that needs replacing with a good experience or there might be something you can do to overcome the fear. Sometimes being alongside a child through the feared thing might be enough.

Bible help

Whoever dwells in the shelter of the Most High will rest in the shadow of the Almighty. I will say of the Lord, 'He is my refuge and my fortress, my God, in whom I trust.' ... You will not fear the terror of night, nor the arrow that flies by day. ... For he will command his angels concerning you to guard you in all your ways.
From Psalm 91

The whole of this psalm is very helpful when dealing with fears. It turns our eyes firmly to the one who is greater than anything we could be afraid of. You could suggest a child learns a verse by heart to say at times when they feel afraid. Alternatively, they could say the Lord's Prayer.

Prayer point

When praying with children, ask God for...

- help with fear
- practical ways to cope with it
- strength to help others who are afraid
- Jesus' protection against the Evil One who always wants to nurture our fear.

Don't pray...

- 'against the power of fear' unless compelled to – they are loaded words
- that the child will be 'brave' or 'tough'.

"For Instance"

I know that my fear was rooted in the Blitz. Born in Chelmsford in March 1945, I was a baby of two weeks old when the 'doodlebug' flying bombs came. The older children in the family held my body down in the pram as my mother pushed me home in the raids.

Fifty years later I asked someone to pray with me to break the fear. That prayer time was painful and frightening in itself but the fear went; the root was axed. A shame I had to wait so long for it to happen. Now when fear threatens, I pray in tongues, as an open acknowledgement of the presence of Jesus who frees us from fear. Or I say the Lord's Prayer: 'Deliver us from evil'.

Further help

Donna Reid Vann, *Stefan's Greatest Fear*, Lion Publishing.

Friendships

Simon Marshall

The concept we know as friendship is a unique mixture of many needs and emotions. For a child, friendship may be about being valued and learning to value others, self-esteem, security and learning to express emotion. However, children are unlikely to think of friends in these terms. Most children view friends in terms of having fun, sharing secrets and games, or having someone to walk home with and sit next to at lunch time. It is fascinating that most children will become (or try to become) part of a friendship group. Adult or child, nobody likes being left out.

The child's need to belong shows itself in many ways. For example, a group of children become a gang or clique and form an identity of their own. This group decides together about what to do or wear or which pop group is the best. Or two children may become inseparable, spending almost all of their time in one another's company to the exclusion of others. These situations can have a profound effect on church groups to which these children come.

The Bible says much about God's view of friendship. At the very beginning, God said, 'It is not good for the man to be alone. I will make a helper suitable for him' (Genesis 2:18). Jesus wept over the death of his friend Lazarus (John 11:35) and befriended Zacchaeus who, we can imagine, had few close friends (Luke 19:1-10). God is concerned with the unloved and the lost, as well as the popular figures. He is in the business of making friends.

Many leaders use the idea of God as our friend to help children grasp his love, care and faithfulness. However, there is a danger of giving a distorted picture. Emphasis on these aspects of God's nature has to be balanced with speaking of him as the almighty, sovereign Lord of all. (As is said of Aslan in the *Narnia* books: God is 'not a tame lion'.)

Chat Box

'No one likes me'

A child who says this may have been hurt by another child and now believes that this is how everyone feels about him. Begin by asking the child why he thinks that no one likes him. What proof does he have? If the child talks about a specific incident you can reassure him that this does not mean that *nobody* likes him. However, be careful not to ignore any wrong that may have been done in this incident. There may be another child who needs to say sorry, or who needs to be disciplined appropriately. If possible, remind him of another friendship: 'But what about Sam? He's your friend, isn't he?'

Of course, there may be a child in a group who is disliked with good reason. A child who always has an unkind word to say or who manages to spoil a game or activity for the rest of the group will quickly become unpopular, and the group will become demotivated. In this case, it is important to try to put the situation right before individual children begin to take the matter into their own hands or leave the group. It is also important to try to find out what is causing this behaviour in the child. Talking to parents early on is important.

'I'm lonely'

It may be that this feeling is shown rather than spoken. You may see that a particular child is left out of group activities by other children or never has a partner for a game. In a group where many of the members go to the same school or live near to each other, a child who does not have that in common with the others may be left out. It may be that the child lacks confidence in making friends. In this case the child may want to be close to a group leader or helper to receive recognition and contact.

A child may voice her loneliness in subtle ways: for example, saying that she doesn't know which group to join when dividing into groups for activities or telling parents that she doesn't know anyone in the group, even after several weeks of attendance. If you know or suspect that a child is lonely, then the best thing that you can offer to the child is friendship. However, you also need to give the child the chance to make friends with others. Deliberately pair children up with someone they might get on with. Introduce a child to others and give them something to do or tell them something that might start a conversation between them. Try including games and activities in your group session which do not require teams or pairs but which allow each child to participate equally.

Advice for children who want to make new friends

Many children in a group may already know each other well, perhaps from school or from a previous church group. So when a child arrives at a group for the first time, he needs to feel quickly that he belongs. It is essential that group leaders continually think about the welcome provided by the group. No child is likely to stay in a group, however good the activities and teaching, if it does not feel a comfortable place to be. The relationships modelled by the leaders are key in helping new members to feel at home and to make friends. It is also important to provide opportunities for new children to make friends. If the session is packed and fast-moving, how much space will there be for friendships to be developed? It is useful to ask a current member of the group to 'look after' a new child and to make sure that he or she knows what is happening throughout the session. Keep in mind that the gospel of Jesus is about welcoming the lost, so that when new children come along you are able to give as much attention to welcoming that child as to the content of the session.

Extra social activities are especially good for new members to feel at home in the group. Perhaps a video night or a trip out somewhere will give them the inroads they need into new friendships.

For a child who wants to make new friends at school, suggest that they ask whoever they sit near in class if they can join in at playtime. Or perhaps they could find a familiar face from church they could talk to. A playground is a big place when you feel alone, so sympathize with the child and promise to pray for them to have courage to join in with someone.

Helping to mend broken friendships

Broken friendships can be very upsetting for both the children involved and the group as a whole. For example, two children who fall out may try to take other children on to their side: 'Don't be friends with her, 'cos we're not talking to her.' In church groups, which rely on sharing of resources, group work and trust, we want to avoid letting broken friendships harm our work and the children involved.

When children fall out, it will often be sorted out very quickly. Don't be too keen to dive in! If the division continues try first to find out the reason, listening to all sides. Act as mediator but try not to dictate what happens by asking the children what they think should happen next. Encourage apology, and encourage them to remember that once 'sorry' has been said, the matter should be over.

Bible help

Do nothing out of selfish ambition or vain conceit, but in humility consider others better than yourselves. Each of you should look not only to your own interests, but also to the interests of others. Your attitude should be the same as that of Christ Jesus: Who, being in very nature God, did not consider equality with God something to be grasped, but made himself nothing, taking the very nature of servant, being made in human likeness. And being found in appearance as a human being, he humbled himself and became obedient to death – even death on a cross!
Philippians 2:3-8

This is a powerful reminder of what our attitude to others should be as we follow Jesus. Following this example will allow newcomers to our groups to feel valued and cared for by the other members.

Or look at:

Psalm 23	God the loving shepherd is always close to us
Romans 8:35-39	We are never cut off from Christ's love
Ephesians 4:2-3	Love and fellowship with others in the church
Ephesians 4:32 – 5:2	Forgiving others as God forgave us

Prayer point

When praying with children about friendship, reassure them that God will never leave them and can always be trusted. Pray for specific needs, for example that a child will be able to find one friend (i.e. setting a realistic target which may be exceeded).

For Instance

Sarah, leader of a children's group, writes:

One week, we got talking about problems we had at school with our friends. Some of the children shared experiences from their own school life. One little girl, Amy, told the group about a little boy who wouldn't be her friend and kept annoying her. Amy talked about how that made her feel angry and hurt. I talked with the whole group about God being a perfect friend who never lets us down. We prayed for Amy and asked God to help her when she was in that situation at school.

TEACHING SESSION: Friends for life

Colossians 3:8-14

Leaders' help

Paul is writing to the Colossian Christians to give them a firm foundation in the truth about Jesus. Other people have been putting round false messages about what it means to live a Christian life. So Paul makes it clear that what matters most is quality of relationships. He talks about what makes relationships bad (verses 8-9), and explains what sort of relationships God's people should have (verses 12-14).

The model for our relationships is God. He loves us, owns us and forgives us. Paul uses the picture of taking off old clothes and putting on new ones to talk about how we get rid of the bad relationship qualities and take on board those which are God-like.

Aim

To help the children learn that as God loves and cares for us, so we should show the same quality of love to those around us.

Way in

For younger children: Bring in a photo of one of your good friends. Describe to the children why that person is your friend. Ask them each to think of a friend and to say what they like about this friend.

For older children: On a large piece of paper (wallpaper or lining paper from a DIY store is good) make life-size outlines of items of clothing by drawing round different children, e.g. trousers, socks, T-shirt, hat, shoes. Ask the children to say what they like about their friends, what they like to do with their friends, etc. Then write these ideas inside the outline, or let the children write if they are able.

Tell it

For younger children: Explain that what God likes best is loving people and being kind to them. He wants us to be the same. Say some kind and unkind phrases which a child might say to a 'friend' based on the qualities in Colossians 3:8-14, e.g. 'You're horrible!' or 'You can play with my trains', or 'I don't like you', or 'Sorry!' If it is something unkind, the children must sit down and put their hands over their mouths. If it's kind, they must repeat the words after you and then jump up in the air.

For older children: Have an old overcoat or similar with some of the relationship qualities from Colossians 3:8-9 pinned to it. Have some other clothes with the qualities from verses 11-14 pinned to them. Wear the overcoat to read verses 8-10. Then take it off and, as you read verses 12-14, put on the 'new' clothes one by one.

Apply it

Ask the children to think of situations in which a friend has shown love or unkindness to them. They could act some of these out. Point out that God's people are supposed to be experts at showing love to others, because they know how much God loves them. That will mean that we don't limit our friends to those we find easiest to get on with.

Respond to God

For younger children: Ask the children to think of something they could do to help a friend, e.g. sharing their toys or including someone in a game. Then pray together to ask God's help in doing these things. Ask the children to name some of their friends. Say a prayer including them all.

For older children: Ask the children to think of a friend who doesn't know Jesus, or who doesn't come to the group. Talk about what could be done to show the friend that God loves them. Pray together about these ideas, perhaps mentioning these friends by name: e.g. the leader says 'Lord, we ask you to help...' and then the children mention the names of their friends.

If time allows, younger and older children could make a card to give to a friend with a message saying 'Thank you for being my friend'.

Section 18

Bullying

Geoff Treasure

Mum and Dad were convinced that something was wrong. When you have put on the first nappy, listened to the first word, and witnessed the first attack of acne, you can tell when things aren't right. Michael had changed over the past month. He was less boisterous, spent more time alone in his bedroom and exhibited mood swings which brought him low for longer periods than high. School was a no-go topic of discussion and, if Michael had his way, a no-go area for him as a pupil. And then one evening Michael let it all out. He was being bullied.

There were no bruises or black eyes. The scars were internal but as real and perhaps more damaging than any physical evidence of a brush with a school bully.

Sadly, school bullies aren't simply characters from children's comics. They are realities. They come in all shapes and sizes and act in a variety of ways. Bullies can shout or whisper, act or merely threaten, be open or secret, damage people or possessions. Sometimes the victims are told clearly why they are the object of bullying; on other occasions they may be left in ignorance. Whether the bully is a loner or the leader of a gang, the damage he or she inflicts can be immense. The results can include fear, anxiety, withdrawal, school phobia, low self-esteem, under-performance and acute unhappiness even to the point of suicide. After all, who cares?

Bullying isn't just an issue for school to deal with. In our church groups, we may well have children who are being bullied at school and we need to be aware and ready to listen. There may be a bully in the group – yes, church children can be bullies! We might be able to help explore the reason for their behaviour and assist them to stop. There may even be bullying happening in the group or club. Hard to believe? Bullying is usually covert and can be happening under our noses.

When it comes to communication about bullying, you may well find that the barriers are up. A child may be scared about what a bully will do to them if they tell someone what is happening. However, where the bullying occurs at school, a child may find a church group leader a safe person to talk to. During a group session, they may casually mention an incident which, in fact, they have not spoken about to anyone else.

Chat Box

'There's a girl at school who's really horrible to me.'

As well as gently finding out more about what has been happening, it is important to ask 'Have you told anyone about it?'

'You can't do anything to stop it.'

If the bullying is taking place in school, the staff there will be very concerned to do something about it. Most schools now have a policy on bullying, can initiate strategies to prevent such antisocial behaviour and will provide support and counselling. Encourage the youngster to share the problem with his or her teacher, pastoral head or some other trusted person. If this fails, encourage the parents to become involved with the school. Experience shows that bullying can be stopped, the bully punished and the bullied protected.

If the bullying is taking place in or around your group sessions, you have a duty to take action yourself. If there is a continuing problem, it is important to take advice from experienced church leaders and to talk to parents as well as hearing what the children involved have to say.

'Talking to you will only make things worse.'

A child may feel trapped by a bully's threats. Talking to someone is the first step in changing the situation – the way out of the trap. The bully wants the other child to keep quiet because they are scared of what will happen if they do tell someone. To stay silent is to let the bully have their own way, while to speak out is to resist them.

'Wouldn't it be best to change schools?'

It has its attractions, putting a distance between the bully and the victim. In reality, it does little to solve the problems. The bully remains to extend his or her terror. The victim has walked away in defeat. It may be hard but, if the victim remains, the experience may enrich and strengthen them. Solve it rather than shake it off.

'Why me?'

Who knows except the bully? The roots may lie in jealousy, low self-esteem, personal problems or even the bully's own experience of being bullied.

Bible help

The Lord is my light and my salvation – whom shall I fear? The Lord is the stronghold of my life – of whom shall I be afraid? ... For in the day of trouble he will keep me safe in his dwelling; he will ... set me high upon a rock. ... Wait for the Lord; be strong and take heart and wait for the Lord.
From Psalm 27

A victim of bullying may find it very hard to believe that God is concerned about their situation. But he is, and he is stronger than any bully. As David acknowledged in this psalm, the problem may not disappear overnight, but we can trust God to deal with it.

Or look at:

2 Kings 6:8-23	Elisha's servant gets a stunning vision of God's protection

Prayer point

God cares for us and wants us to throw all those things that bother us on to him, so there is every encouragement to pray about the problem.

With the child, try to pray for:

- the bully – for the causes of the bullying behaviour to be cleared up
- the victim – for courage to stand up to the bully and share the problem with others
- the problem – that it will come to an end.

"For Instance"

One moment Joanna had been 'in' with the rest of the group; the next, she was 'out'. Friendship had ended and bullying began. It was very subtle. There was isolation in the playground, dirty looks across the classroom, pushing and shoving in the corridor, notes left on her desk, and bags which went missing. She decided to share the problem with her tutor. The tutor spoke to the other girls involved in the bullying before bringing them and Joanna together. Views were exchanged, misconceptions cleared up and suspicions removed. For all concerned it was the end of one chapter and the beginning of another.

Further help

Zoë Crutchley and Veronica Parnell, *Bullying – Sorted!*, Scripture Union.

Kidscape, 152 Buckingham Palace Road, London, SW1W 9TR (Tel: 0171 730 3300) – a charity aiming to teach children how to keep safe before they become victims.

Anti Bullying Campaign, 10 Borough High Street, London, SE1 9QQ (Tel: 0171 378 1446) – a support group for parents and children which produces a free fact sheet and other publications.

ChildLine (Tel: 0800 1111) – a free 24-hour helpline for children to ring. They also produce helpful leaflets on bullying.

TEACHING SESSION: Bullying

2 Kings 6:8-23

Leaders' help

The Arameans (Syrians) were neighbours and long-term enemies of Israel. But God protected his people from their attacks through his man, Elisha. This incident gives a startling picture of God's protection. Elisha's servant was terrified by the sight of the surrounding enemy, but Elisha shows him that God's power is much greater, even if it is usually unseen. Amazingly, the Arameans are not killed, but given a feast – a sign of friendship – and sent home. The attacks stop.

God still protects his people, and he still uses human agents to bring that about. God's power is still greater than any enemy's, even though it may be invisible to the human eye. And God still has a radically different view about how enemies should be treated.

Remember: *Some of the children will have direct experience of bullying, either as bullies or being bullied. Plan how to give the children an opportunity to talk with someone at the end of this session.*

Aim

To help children understand that God is greater than any bully and he can give us courage to face any situation.

Way in

Show the children a duvet. Ask them to suggest how it feels to be completely surrounded by it. Repeat this with other items, e.g. water, wire-wool, people, mud, balls (as in a play ball-room). Finish by asking how it would feel to be surrounded by people who do not like you.

Point out that when people are nasty to someone and bully them that person can feel trapped. It's as if they are surrounded by something horrible and they can't escape. That's a very bad feeling. Explain that we're going to find out how that situation can be changed.

Tell it

Choose children to be Elisha, his servant, the king of Israel and the Aramean army. Begin by explaining that the Arameans were enemies of Israel. They kept trying to attack the Israelites. But each time God warned his man, Elisha, of the attack and Elisha told the king of Israel so he was ready. Then the Arameans decided that what they needed to do was to attack Elisha.

Tell the rest of the story (2 Kings 6:14-23) with the children acting out what happens as you go along. Pause to help them do this. With older children, you could read the passage directly from a child-friendly translation. With younger children, it will need a little adaptation.

Apply it

Older children: In groups of three or four, ask the children to act out a situation in which one person is being bullied. Encourage them to think of things they might know about from school, or their own friends. Talk together about what could have been said, by whom and to whom. What could have been done, by whom and to whom?

Younger children: Sit in a huddle and surround the whole group in duvets, blankets, pillows, etc. so you are all cosy. Explain that just as God protected Elisha, he promises to shelter us in his love. Blankets surround us and keep us warm, even though outside it may feel very cold and uncomfortable. In the same way God surrounds us with his love, even if bullies are making our life horrible. And he is more powerful than any human being.

All ages: Talk briefly about what children should do if they or someone they know is being bullied. Encourage them to speak to someone, perhaps you, and to pray to God for trust and help. Explain that it is important to do something about it, however hard or scary that may seem, to show that it is not right. How can we respond to bullying in more positive ways, like the people of Israel did?

Respond to God

Explain that God is still stronger than anything or anyone who might threaten to hurt us. We can't see him, but he is with us. Pray together for people who are bullied and for those who do the bullying. Older children might like to write prayers which they or others could use when they are being bullied.

Section 20

Abuse

David and Pauline Pearson

There are different forms of abuse, including physical (e.g. hitting, shaking, biting), emotional (e.g. humiliating, denying love and affection), sexual (any sexual activity that an adult – or young person – undertakes with a child by force, coercion or persuasion), and neglect (failing to meet a child's basic needs). Males and females abuse, and many more children are hurt by people they know well than by strangers.

The church has a general responsibility to act if abuse comes to light and to protect children, as far as possible, from being abused within the church. All churches should have their own child protection document or be working under guidelines from their diocese or supervisory body. This policy should set out good practice for working with children, including how to minimize the possibility of abuse occurring. It should also explain how to respond if a child discloses abuse. Your response will be crucial. If you do not have a policy, start to locate one immediately.

For example: Sarah, aged 9, is a regular attender at your group. She used to be a bright, bubbly girl – but not any more. She seems isolated from the group, who tease her. There are dark shadows under her eyes and she seems anxious and fearful all the time. She's always going to the toilet and often complains of vague pains. When you ask her if she's told her mum, she looks panicky and says, 'Oh, I couldn't.' Surprised, you say, 'Your mum seems very nice and your new stepdad, too.' Sarah's face drops and she walks away...

This week when she arrives early, you chat with her and say, 'Sometimes when we're worried, it's helpful to talk to someone about it.' Suddenly Sarah flings herself into your arms, sobbing. She discloses that her stepdad has been touching her bottom and hurting her. He said that she mustn't tell anyone, but she can't keep it a secret any more.

Sexual abuse is only one kind of abuse that children can experience. In our society, sexual abuse is a criminal offence. In God's eyes it is sin. Matthew 18:6 expresses God's view of those who hurt children. He can see how a child's innocence and simple trust in God and people can be destroyed, and how the child becomes angry, fearful and confused, hating themselves and becoming more vulnerable.

Top tips

– for when a child wants to talk about abuse

General points

- Don't promise confidentiality. Explain that you might need to tell someone else.
- Don't probe or prompt with any questions.
- Listen with acceptance (however unlikely the story may sound).
- Keep calm.
- Look at the child directly.
- Be honest.
- Even when a child has broken a rule, they are not to blame for the abuse.
- Be aware that the child may have been threatened.
- Never push for information.

Helpful things to say or show

- 'I believe you' (or show acceptance of what the child says).
- 'I am glad you have told me.'
- 'It's not your fault.'
- 'I will help you.'

Avoid saying

- 'Why didn't you tell anyone before?'
- 'You should have said no.'
- 'I can't believe it!'
- 'Are you sure this is true?'
- 'Why? How? When? Who? Where?'
- 'I'm shocked, don't tell anyone else.'

Advice on praying

Encourage the child that they have done the right thing in coming to talk to you about what has happened. They have been very brave. They are not to blame for what someone else has done to them. Ask if they would like you to pray with them. Pray asking that God will bring them comfort and strength in order to deal with what might follow their disclosure. Remind them that God is not angry with them but he is very sad about what has happened to them.

Concluding the conversation

• Again, reassure the child that they were right to tell you and that you believe them.

• Let the child know what you are going to do next and that you will let them know what happens. (You might have to consider contacting social services or the police to prevent the child returning home if you consider them to be in immediate, serious risk of further abuse.)

• Immediately refer the matter to someone appropriately qualified, following your child protection policy. This might be your church leader or youth and children's work supervisor.

After the conversation

Make notes as soon as possible (preferably within an hour of the conversation), writing down exactly what the child said, when he or she said it and what was happening immediately beforehand (e.g. a description of the activity). Record dates and times of these events and when you made the record. Keep all handwritten notes, even if you subsequently type them up. Store notes in a secure place.

For Instance

Toby's mum and dad split up and his mum was left looking after the children. Sometimes she would get very angry with them and one day Toby was badly beaten. He told his Sunday School teacher who took him to hospital. The doctor and a social worker were very kind to Toby and they also talked to his mum. Things are better now that Toby's mum has someone she can talk to when she's worried about things. And Toby knows he can always speak to someone at church who listens to children.

Chat Box

These sample answers illustrate the kind of language you might use. Details of the answers you give will depend on the situation.

'Have I been naughty? He said I mustn't tell.'

'You have done the right thing in telling. It's never naughty to tell grown-ups about bad secrets.'

'Why did my mum do those things to me?'

'Sometimes people do things that are wrong because bad things have happened to them too. They need very special help to make sure they stop.'

'What will happen to my stepdad now I've told you?'

'I'm not sure, but a social worker and police officer will be asking lots of questions. It might be that he is not allowed to live with you for a while so that you don't get hurt anymore.'

Further help

The Churches Child Protection Advisory Service (part of PCCA Christian Child Care) PCCA, PO Box 133, Swanley, Kent, BR8 7UQ (Tel: 01322 667207/660011). PCCA advises and supports churches on issues of child abuse and child protection, providing workpacks and training materials.

NSPCC, 42 Curtain Road, London, EC2A 3NH (helpline: 0800 800 500) – provides useful leaflets on abuse and prevention.

Kidscape, 152 Buckingham Palace Road, London, SW1W 9TR – a charity campaigning for children's safety.

ChildLine (Tel: 0800 1111) – a free 24-hour helpline for children. They also produce leaflets on abuse.

Your local Social Services department. Look for the number in your local phone book. You can make an appointment to speak to a social worker about a child protection issue.

Your denominational offices (e.g. Diocesan Children's Adviser) will put you in touch with whoever is responsible for child protection policies.

Section 21

Adoption and fostering

David and Pauline Pearson

Children who have been adopted want to feel the same as their peers. For some who are well established in their adoptive families this may be true most or even all of the time. But others may feel particularly insecure and have a sense of rejection by their birth parents. They may not know much about their family of origin. They might not know their family's medical history.

Children may also come to the group having been placed with foster carers. This could be because they need short-term care during a family crisis (e.g. hospitalization) or because they have been neglected or abused. These children may need lots of love and patience. They may be angry and aggressive; they may seek reassurance but hate to be touched. Talk things through with their carers and relay any concerns to them.

It's important for all adopted or fostered children to know that they are not a mistake but a very special part of God's plan. Our acceptance of them may be especially important.

Many learning activities in published group materials relate to families. Adapt or replace any which will be difficult for children in your group who do not live with or know their birth parents: for example, references to family likenesses, family history or 'when you were a baby'. Watch out for the way you speak about families as well. Listen to the names the children themselves use of their carers and use the same ones.

Bible help

To all who received [Jesus], to those who believed in his name, he gave the right to become children of God – children born not of natural descent, nor of human decision or a husband's will, but born of God.
John 1:12-13

Adoption into God's family is a picture used several times in the Bible to describe becoming a Christian. An adopted or fostered child may feel that, to their parents, they were a mistake or unwanted. Whatever the truth or otherwise of that feeling, there is no question that God wants them as part of his family.

Or look at:

Romans 8:15-17 We are adopted as God's children with a great inheritance coming

Chat Box

'Why don't you live with your real mum and dad?'

'Why did they give you away?'

In some groups, children will want to ask questions about another child's adoption. Take your lead from the child concerned. If they are happy to talk about it, then this can be a good thing for the group. If the child wants to close the subject, move on.

Where you want to give a general answer, you might say that sometimes a parent will know that they are just not able to give their child all the love and care that they need. It's a hard decision for them to make but sometimes they have to ask social workers to find a family who will be able to do that.

For Instance

Nicola, now aged 30, was adopted at three weeks old. She has always known she was adopted, and doesn't feel any different from other people because of it. She sees her adoption as a very positive thing – as a second chance to give her the love and security that she could not have received from her birth parents.

Five years ago Nicola gave a talk in church about being chosen by God. She was able to use the example of her own adoption to show what it means to be adopted into God's family. Just as her adoptive parents made a choice to commit themselves to her for life, so she was able to talk about the commitment that God makes to each of us in love.

One issue meant a lot for Nicola. During her training as a nursery nurse, Nicola was learning the importance of the first three weeks of 'bonding' between parent and child. She found herself asking the question: 'Who was looking after *me* during those early weeks of my life?' Her church youth group leader pointed her to Psalm 139:13-16, which helped her to realize that, supremely, it was God who had been caring for her.

Section 22

Home – arguments

Linda Stone

How many families arrive at church having had a thoroughly stressful time trying to sort everyone out to get there? As group leaders we may be the first people to meet children arriving after an argument at home, whether it was about clothing, breakfast, cleaning teeth or whether they wanted to go to church at all. It is always good to start with an activity which thoroughly involves the children, whether it is active or calming in mood, to help them leave all those things behind.

We might also hear about a long-running argument with parents, siblings or friends. Or we might hear about a row which was not resolved and which has left the child still feeling hurt. A child in the group might be the one who causes the arguments in their home. If they are argumentative at home, that will spill over into our time with them.

Where two or more children from a family are in the same group, any tension between them will be carried over into the group. That may be reflected in their body language or openly in words. You may need to plan how to keep siblings involved in different groups to minimize the opportunity for backbiting.

Arguments are a natural part of life, but to say only this would be to belittle how it feels for the child involved. In most cases our role is to be peacemakers, peace-givers and reassurers.

Top tips

Dealing with arguments

- An intermediary is always useful. Can you be that person? This might take you into a relationship out of your group context.
- Encourage the child to apologize and make up as soon as possible. Sympathize as to how hard this is. Explain that saying sorry first is very hard but is the bravest and best thing to do.
- Try to get the child to see both sides of the argument.
- Remember that it is easier to reason with a calm child. Allow time and space for cooling off after a row.
- If one child is deliberately provoking another, encourage the other child to ignore it as much as possible. Quite a lot of provocation is done simply to get a reaction; encourage the child not to give the provoker this satisfaction!

Bible help

But the wisdom that comes from heaven is first of all pure; then peace-loving, considerate, submissive, full of mercy and good fruit, impartial and sincere. Peacemakers who sow in peace raise a harvest of righteousness.
James 3:17-18

The wise approach is to love peace. Arguments lead to hurt and on to more arguments. If we go for peace then the results will be good things for everyone concerned.

Or look at:

Matthew 5:38-41	Jesus teaches about dealing with those who wrong us
Proverbs 15:1	The different results of gentle and harsh words

Prayer point

Suggest a child asks God for forgiveness for any wrong actions or words on their side. And pray for the courage to forgive the person with whom they have fallen out.

“For Instance”

I remember a friend with whom I used to spend more time arguing than playing. We would argue about other friends ‘taking you away’ and whether or not ‘you like me more than her’. I still hear girls in the playground saying the same things. I remember a solid piece of advice which a dinner lady gave me in the middle of a big falling-out. She advised me to make sure I was never in the wrong so my friend could never accuse me of something and be right with that accusation. It certainly stopped me from trying to take revenge!

Section 23

Long-term illness

Jackie Cray

Children generally react to a long-term condition in one of three ways. They may...

- try to hide the condition
- overcompensate to show that there is nothing wrong with them
- make use of the condition to attract attention or get their own way.

Be aware of a child's response and help them to handle it well (see **Top tips**).

Remember that there is a difference between an ongoing condition and long-term illness. Having a condition may mean that someone has to deal with a number of physical or other side effects, but they may not actually be ill.

'You have no idea how it feels!'

Some children face long-term conditions like diabetes or epilepsy with the need for on-going medication, diet and treatment. Others face terminal illnesses with the implications of physical or mental deterioration but also with the possibility of preparation for an end (and a new beginning).

Whether a child is dealing with a treatable illness, a long-term condition or a terminally ill relative, they need to be given space and permission to express what they feel. Initially they may not even be able to describe their feelings or have the appropriate language to do so. At this stage they need to know that, as far as possible, our love and acceptance of them is unconditional. Those who are closest to the child often bear the brunt of the child's discomfort with themselves or others. Someone like a church group leader can often provide the 'safe' place which the child needs to begin to explore how they feel about their illness, themselves and God.

Chat Box

'Why me?'

'Do I have to take this medicine/have this injection?'

'Is there any treatment?'

'Will the treatment be painful?'

'What difference will the treatment make?'

'Am I going to die and will it hurt?'

In answering children's questions, always be prayerful, wise and honest. Don't be afraid to say, 'I don't know.' A child needs someone to take time to explain the things that can be explained: the reasons why a treatment needs to be given and the options available if treatment isn't given. If the child is in need of information but is not getting it from their parents or medical staff, you might ask the child if they would like you to talk to their parents on their behalf.

Top tips

When a child in the group has a long-term condition or illness

- Help the child to learn when to ask for help or for allowances to be made. At the same time, encourage them to overcome self-imposed limitations by trying to live positively and creatively.
- Find a balance between ignoring the problem and exaggerating it.
- Find creative ways of helping the child achieve goals that might have seemed impossible.
- Help to build up the child's self-esteem (see pages 8-9).
- Be matter-of-fact about the illness; it is something to be dealt with, not an issue for sympathy or hero worship. The child needs to think of themselves as normal.
- Be aware of prescribed drugs. Clarify with the parent and the child what responsibility they want you to take for keeping drugs safe, or reminding the child to take them. Remember to be discreet.
- Always respect the privacy and dignity of the child. Do not have conversations with other people over their heads; encourage the parent to allow the child to be involved in discussions about their condition.

Bible help

Is any one of you in trouble? You should pray. Is anyone happy? Sing songs of praise. Is any one of you sick? Call the elders of the church to pray over you and anoint you with oil in the name of the Lord. And the prayer offered in faith will make you well; the Lord will raise you up.
James 5:13-15

Prayer is the right response to any form of suffering or sickness. Whatever we are experiencing, God is concerned. And he will answer our prayer, though this may not necessarily be in the form of physical healing.

Prayer point

When praying with a child, always ask what they would like you to pray for and explain what you are going to do, e.g. 'I'm going to ask God to...' Invite the child to focus on Jesus. After you've prayed, ask the child how they are feeling. Often they will have experienced something from God themselves during the prayer time. Assure them that God loves them and knows their needs. Remind them that he sometimes answers our prayers in unexpected ways. *Always* look for ways of building up the child's faith.

"For Instance"

Josie's story

I can honestly say that I didn't handle my condition so well when I was younger. I ran off and hid every time my parents were to give me my injection, because I knew it would hurt. I suppose the main things that helped were: my big sister who was very understanding, the support of my family and friends, and knowing that people were praying for me and with me. I've never felt I've been treated as different, which is great. Honesty mattered a lot to me, whether from doctors or parents. I needed to know why something was happening – why the increase in medication, for example? Once it had been explained to me and I understood why it was necessary, I could cope much better.

"For Instance"

Katy's story

As a child and into my early teens, I was quite often in trouble for not obeying instructions which I couldn't remember being given. This happened at home, at school and at after-school clubs. I remember the frustration and anger at being told off for disobeying when I knew I hadn't. Sometimes I was even accused of lying as a result. I felt angry and resentful as I was punished for something I hadn't done. Often I felt isolated from my peers.

But worst of all was the nagging self-doubt that maybe there was something wrong with me. If everyone else thought I had ignored what had been said to me, and I couldn't remember it, then maybe I really was stupid or mad. I had no idea there was a physical cause for this problem. What no one realized was that I was having a kind of seizure where I would 'zone out' of conversation and miss vital information. At the age of fourteen I began having a more visible form of seizure and was diagnosed as having epilepsy. It was only years later that a neurologist suggested to me that it might have been the cause of my childhood problems.

With medical treatment and more understanding, I have been able to overcome most of the problems epilepsy causes. What I wish, though, is that someone had believed me as a child and taken time to find out why I was behaving as I did.

Further help

There are support organizations for people with specific conditions and their carers. For information and addresses contact a GP's surgery or Citizens' Advice Bureau.

Section 24

Divorce and separation

Jenny Hyatt

One of the worst situations any child can experience is the break-up of their family. Not only does it mean the separation of the two most important people in their lives, but it can also mean the loss of their 'support base' as they move home to be with one parent or the other, or spend their time shuffling between the two. Acrimonious custody battles may be raging around them; you may glimpse some of these tensions in the way they are delivered to or collected from your group by different parents. Establishing which parent you as leader should have prime contact with can be like treading on egg shells!

Other 'hidden' factors may also affect children of divorce. Their quality of lifestyle may be affected: suddenly there is less money to go round as, unknown to them, they have 'dropped' a socio-economic category in the process of their parents' divorce. Shopping with friends at weekends isn't much fun if they can't afford anything. The pattern of their week may change too. They may get little parental time for five days, but then have full attention from one parent all weekend.

Within the group, you will probably notice a variety of reactions in children going through a divorce or separation. Many of these will be similar to those caused by bereavement. Emotions will be very near the surface: there may be sudden floods of tears, violent mood swings or angry outbursts for no apparent reason. Other children will try hard to suppress their emotions, withdrawing into themselves and hanging back from the group as a whole. Conflicts within the group may arouse particular fears for them: they have seen where arguments can lead, and they don't like the consequences.

Lack of concentration within the group can also be a problem. The child staring into space who didn't hear your question probably has her mind fixed on her home situation. And uncertainty about weekend custody arrangements may make it very hard to commit to future trips or outings your group may be organizing.

Chat Box

'It must be all my fault.'

Children often blame themselves for the break-up of their parents' marriage. If only they had been better behaved, more helpful, less troublesome, maybe dad wouldn't have left... You need to help them see that their parents' problems are their parents' problems, and that nothing they could have done (or not done) would have changed the way their parents feel about each other.

'Will Daddy leave me as well as Mummy?'

'Has Mum stopped loving me?'

The departure of one parent can create huge insecurity for the child: what happens if the other parent leaves too, or gets ill, or dies...? And for the child, the absent parent's departure can be interpreted as a termination of love. Try to reassure the child that, however their parents feel about each other, they will *always* go on loving their child, and will always be there for them. The parent who has left home is probably missing their children as much as (if not more than) their children are missing them, and will be finding the absence extremely painful.

'How can I go on loving Daddy when Mummy hates him so much?'

Underneath all the personal anger and emotion of this trauma, parents expect – and usually want – their children to go on loving *both* of them, just as they will each continue to love their children. Try to help the child not to take sides, even if they have their own thoughts about who is to blame for the situation.

The child may also be tempted to play one parent off against the other ('Mum didn't want me to come on the outing, but Dad said it was OK'). Don't get drawn into dangerous games like this where your own integrity with both parents is compromised.

'I've asked God to get Mum and Dad back together again.'

This isn't a wrong thing for a child to be praying, but gently point out that if they don't get back together, it doesn't mean that God has stopped loving them or their mum or dad. Don't *ever* offer glib reassurance like 'It'll be all right; Mum and Dad will work it out' or 'God's told me that your mum and dad will get back together again'. False hopes can cause incalculable damage to children later on.

Top tips

• Let the child tell you as much or as little about the situation as they want.

• Keep confidences, especially if the parents are members of your own church.

• Allow for lapses of attention, uncertainty, mood swings.

• Don't encourage the child to take sides against one parent.

• Remember that the factors leading to divorce are very complex: the child's point of view may not be the whole story.

• Don't be judgemental. Your role as leader is not to debate with the child about the rights or wrongs of divorce, but to provide unconditional support for them as they live through it.

• Make every effort to get your relationships right with *both* parents, if possible.

• Keep reminding the child of God's love for them.

Bible help

Are not five sparrows sold for two pennies? Yet not one of them is forgotten by God. Indeed the very hairs of your head are all numbered. Don't be afraid; you are worth more than many sparrows.
Luke 12:6-7

In the middle of a family break-up a child or adult will probably feel God has forgotten them or perhaps even hates them. These verses show that those feelings don't reflect the true situation. In fact, every detail about us matters to God. We are worth a great deal to him, however it feels.

Or look at:

Genesis 21:8-21	Hagar and Ishmael – God's care and concern for a lone parent family
Psalm 68:5-6	God's care for the fatherless, widows and the lonely
Matthew 7:9-11	Human fathers love their children; God's love is even greater

Prayer point

God is always there for us to talk to/shout at/offload onto. If you are praying with a child, give them plenty of time to express all the worries or anxieties that they are feeling; your example of listening and reassurance will be tangible evidence of God's love for them.

"For Instance"

Mandy's parents divorced when she was six years old. Her dad stayed at home, while she and her younger brother moved with mum into her stepfather's house. Because her mum's affair had happened within the local church, it made it very difficult for Mandy and her brother to keep going there. And besides, it was all God's fault for letting the relationship happen in the first place, wasn't it? So after a while she stopped going to Junior Church and lost touch with her friends.

Mandy was instinctively defensive of any attacks on her mother but also very concerned about her dad's unhappiness. She wanted to make things all right for him, as well as for her mum. But the effort screwed her up in knots. As she approached adolescence she developed tummy pains at school, and couldn't eat properly. Her school work suffered, and she never felt able to join friends for sleepovers or trips away which would mean leaving mum on her own.

Gradually, as she grew up, she began to relax about trying to 'parent' her own parents. She realized that after the break-up, her parents were coping with their new situations in different ways and were gradually becoming stronger people. She now has a healthy relationship with both parents. And although she wouldn't call herself a Christian by any means, she's stopped being angry with God.

Further help

Carolyn Nystrom, *Mike's Lonely Summer,* Lion Publishing.

Roger Smith and John Bradford, *Children and Divorce,* Church House Publishing.

Family Mediators Association (FMA), 1 Wyvil Court, Wyvil Road, London SW8 2TG (E-mail: info@familymediators.co.uk) – information about helping children experiencing divorce and new family situations.

Section 25

New families

Sue Collinson

This section looks at the joys and pains that occur when a new family emerges from an old one; either through a child's parents forming new relationships after divorce or death or through the birth of a baby. Change can bring great joy and relief. However, there is no change as disturbing as a new family structure. We, as adults, feel insecurity, jealousy, or competitiveness in our close relationships and we can expect nothing more or less from the children in our care.

God is concerned because he is a God of love and relationship. He has put us in families to experience, learn and demonstrate his own unconditional love. Within families we develop a concept of trust that will pave the way for all our future relationships.

Remarriage

After a traumatic event like divorce or death, the formation of a new relationship is a challenge for all family members to face. However, in that setting, a new marriage can be seen as a very positive thing for all concerned. Children see their parent finding happiness and younger children particularly may be glad of a reduction in levels of tension.

Remarriage and new partnerships are increasingly common in society, but still relatively unusual in many churches. A child may feel different from others in the group because of having two mothers or two fathers. This is particularly significant for children over seven for whom peer acceptance is paramount. Other children can be strangely proud of their situation. As one child said: 'I've got four families, now.'

The nature of the relationship between the divorced couple will continue to have an impact. As members of the church we can help by guarding our tongues and giving non-judgemental support and acceptance to the new family. Access arrangements may well lead to irregular group attendance. The child needs leaders to be understanding and accepting.

Children will act to protect themselves from further pain. This could show itself in not wanting to rock the boat, lying low, being unobtrusive, distant, uncomplaining so that people don't get angry or upset. As with any domestic upheaval, a child may show lack of concentration or become easily distracted. (Though if they are acting in these ways at home, they may feel it is safe to act in the opposite manner at church!) Younger children can show great distress when arguments occur or tension is felt.

If there are obvious tensions between the child and the new parent, listening is invaluable. However, the new adult relationship must never be compromised. Children need space to settle into the new relationship. For an adolescent it may take years.

Names are important. Check what surnames the children and the adults involved are now using. Write them down if you think you might forget. Also find out what names the children are using to refer to new step-parents so you can use them too. Ask the children early to save embarrassment later on.

Chat Box

'No one else has two dads.'

In response, you could talk about different types of families and situations, e.g. foster children, children living with grandparents, children where dad works away, changes in families due to death or divorce. There is no 'normal' or 'right' pattern.

New baby

A new baby's arrival is something to celebrate as a church family. The joy of a new life given by the Creator God vividly reminds us of his love. But not-so-positive emotions also arise, particularly in siblings of a new baby. It is important not to ignore the negative aspects of the demanding newcomer's impact on the rest of the family.

There may be a sense of betrayal ('Mummy said I was her favourite little boy') or loss ('I didn't want to go to the park, I wanted to go swimming like we used to'). Children can be aggressively jealous and show this by pinching, hitting or scratching the new baby. They tend to feel insecure, which will usually show itself in what is seen as attention-seeking behaviour. Remember these reactions are normal. With time they will start to adjust. The church group can be an important part of life which stays the same through the new baby's arrival.

Top tips

When a family in the group is expecting a new baby

• Help prepare by talking about the forthcoming birth.

• When the baby is born celebrate as a group, giving lots of positive affirmation to the older child. A card or present could be made for the whole family.

• Be positive! Talk about the new baby as an individual with needs and a personality: 'Yes he's here, I know it's hard, but think what you can do with your brother when...'

• The child may be feeling a lack of 'quality' time at home. Give them some of yours. Listen and remember that small children understand far more than they can articulate.

• Don't overdo it. The church group may be a place where the child wants to get away from continual baby talk.

• A leader could help mum or dad to have time with their older child or children by helping to fix up babysitting.

Bible help

Fear not for I have redeemed you; I have summoned you by name; you are mine. When you pass through the waters, I will be with you; and when you pass through the rivers they will not sweep over you. ... For I am the Lord, your God, the Holy One of Israel, your Saviour ... you are precious and honoured in my sight...
Isaiah 43:1-4

God's words to Israel in exile apply to all his people facing difficult circumstances. Whatever family changes take place, each individual is known completely by God and very precious to him.

Prayer point

Where a new baby is expected, pray for it with the older child, even before it is born. Ask God to care for it and protect it. This helps the older child to be involved in caring for it from the start.

"For Instance"

Melanie's stepchildren live with their mother, but spend every other weekend with Melanie and their father. The children call her by her name, never by 'Mummy', and when they are out together she always tries to make it clear to people they meet who she is. Once somebody asked Melanie about 'her son' when he was sitting next to her. She laughingly explained what the situation really was, sensing the shock of anxiety running through him, but she felt him gradually relax as he examined her reaction.

Melanie's stepchildren love talking with her about 'Mummy' and about the things they have been doing at home. It's almost as if they are trying to connect together the two places in which they live out their lives. When friends ask the children about their home life, they visibly relax and enjoy telling them about it. But some of Melanie's friends feel uncomfortable to ask, as if somehow this will hurt Melanie; as a result the children are noticeably more tense.

Acceptance is hugely important, too. Melanie remembers feeling relieved and impressed when one of the children's workers at the church she attended came up to her 7-year-old stepdaughter, took her by the hand, called her by name and coaxed her off to the children's Sunday group as if she were there every week and had been going to church for years. It helped her stepdaughter to feel that she belonged there, whatever her home situation might be.

Further help

Jan Godfrey, *Sam's New Baby,* Scripture Union.

National Stepfamily Association UK, 3rd Floor Chapel House, 18 Hatton Place, London EC1N 8RU (Tel: 0171 209 2460).

Family Mediators Association (FMA), 1 Wyvil Court, Wyvil Road, London SW8 2TG (E-mail: info@familymediators.co.uk) – information about helping children experiencing divorce and new family situations.

Gingerbread, 1617 Clerkenwell Close, London EC1R 0AA (Tel: 0171 336 8183; E-mail: general_enquiry@gingerbread.org.uk) – lone parents' association.

Other agencies that can help:

• social services, particularly under-eights' advisors

• health professionals, e.g. GPs, health visitors.

TEACHING SESSION: God made families

Genesis 35:23-26; 37:2-4

Leaders' help

The story of Joseph and his brothers is one of the few Bible stories well known in secular culture, largely due to Andrew Lloyd Webber. The show *Joseph and his Amazing Technicolor Dreamcoat* could give you lots more material for this session – use your imagination!

For some in your group, their family might already have split up; for others they might currently be in the midst of difficult times; while for others, their family might be a wonderful and happy thing. This session assumes that all the group will have at some stage experienced some argument or disagreement with brothers, sisters or parents, whether recently or in the past. Be sensitive to individual situations as far as you are aware of them.

Aim

To help the children realize that God understands and cares when our families go through stressful times.

Way in

Look at the list of names in Genesis 35:23-26. Create a family tree for Joseph. You could do this by cutting out paper-chain people and snipping them at the correct intervals for the different groups of brothers. The children could colour their clothes and stick them on to a large sheet of paper, putting Jacob at the top as father, with his different wives on the next row, and with the correct sons underneath them. Write on all the names.

Discuss with the group what things were different in that family (e.g. more than one wife, lots of children). See if anyone can remember all the names!

Tell it

Use the family tree poster as a visual aid to tell the story of Jacob and his family. If the children are familiar with the musical, they might know much of the complete story as told in Genesis 37–45. However, try to focus on the first four verses of chapter 37. Joseph's brothers hated him because they were jealous of the special attention their father paid to him.

Apply it

Bring in a cake or something nice to eat and divide it up for the group to share. However, make one piece much bigger than the others and hand it to a leader or one of the children, making a big fuss of them. How did the rest of the group feel about not getting a fair slice? Explain that this was a bit like how it was for Joseph and his brothers. Alternatively, try to get hold of three similar items of clothing – perhaps two fairly ordinary or tatty T-shirts and one really splendid one. Describe the situation: it was as if Jacob had given Joseph the really super T-shirt and the others either ordinary or tatty shirts. This had made the brothers really jealous.

Ask whether the children have ever been jealous of anyone in their family. Do they ever feel like they are hard done by?

Hold up a large card or sheet of paper, on which you have written the words from Philippians 2:3. Explain that God doesn't want us to be jealous of others but to live in harmony, thinking of others more than we think of ourselves. Perhaps your group could learn the verse together.

Respond to God

Pray a 'teaspoon' prayer (Thank you, Sorry, Please – TSP!), either individually or as a whole group:

- **Thank you** for our families, especially for ...
- **Sorry** for the times when we provoke our families, especially when ...
- **Please** help us to be good family members, especially ...

Death and loss

Jill Pauling

Any loss can be devastating. Bereavement, especially bereavement through death, is one of the most traumatic emotions that any child has to face. Recent studies have shown that, if unrecognized and untreated, grief may show itself in chronic depression, fear or even physical symptoms for many years. Any adult involved with a child who has experienced the death of a friend or relative can become part of the recovery process. An informed and caring leader, reacting sensitively and sensibly, can be invaluable.

We need to overcome the taboo of talking or thinking about death and start to understand the needs of grieving children. We don't have to be experts but we do need to know that 'shielding' a child from the reality of death by telling half-truths and excluding them from grieving rituals can be damaging. The child does not need to be told to 'cheer up' or 'put a brave face on it', but rather needs to be encouraged to realize that giving expression to their grief is both normal and healthy.

Grief is expressed in many different ways. Children may show anger, aggression, feelings of isolation, withdrawn or sad behaviour or sudden mood swings. Or they may show no outward emotional reaction at all.

The recently bereaved child needs to feel part of a group. They need a safe place to be themself – the same person that they were last week – but they also need the understanding and comfort of a group of friends who have been appropriately prepared and briefed.

Helping the group when a child has been bereaved

The other children in the group will want to ask questions and will need reassurance. Most children do not have barriers or inhibitions. They need simple, direct and, above all, truthful explanations.

- Sit comfortably in a circle.
- You may find it easier to talk without the grieving child present but not necessarily so. Take your lead from the bereaved child. Sensitive, open-ended questions will determine whether the child wants to share or talk.
- Give a clear, simple explanation of the circumstances surrounding the bereavement. Emphasize that these were unusual – to deal with children's fears that the same thing might happen to them.
- Explain that the grieving child will need space but also to feel included in conversations and activities.
- Say that prying, personal questions are not appropriate but that neither should they avoid mentioning the dead person.
- In the rest of the group time, have a healthy mixture of laughter and quieter activities.
- If possible, have a quiet area with an adult available for any child who wants to talk further.

You may decide to have a session looking at the issue of death together (see page 45), especially if someone well known to the whole group has died. Making individual cards, compiling a memory book, planting a shrub or tree, raising a small amount of money for a named charity or sharing memories of the person who has died can all help the grieving process. No one should be forced to discuss death or attend grieving rituals such as funerals. On the other hand a child or group may find it helpful to attend a funeral or service of thanksgiving.

Stages of grief

A bereaved child will probably go through the following stages of grief:

Stage 1: Shock and disbelief. A very young child will often expect their loved one to reappear. This stage may go on for weeks or months. Apathy, withdrawal, calmness, numbness and visible distress are all symptomatic of this stage.

Stage 2: A storm of feelings which may include anger, aggression, anxiety, guilt and fear. This stage requires particularly sensitive handling as the strength of the emotion often makes the child difficult to manage within the group.

Stage 3: Gradual acceptance of the death and a willingness to move on.

Any of the above stages may be revisited out of sequence.

Bible help

The Lord is faithful to all his promises, and he is merciful in all his acts. He helps those who are in trouble; he lifts those who have fallen.
Psalm 145:13-14 *(Good News Bible)*

God has a special concern for people in trouble. He understands the hurt, anxiety, sense of loss and fear when someone close to us dies. He may seem distant and remote from death but, in Jesus, he has become fully involved: experiencing death and dealing with it.

Or look at:

Psalm 139	God is personally involved with each individual
Revelation 21:3-4	God's promise of a future with him and without tears
Romans 8:38-39	Nothing can separate us from Christ's love
John 3:16	The promise of everlasting life
John 11	Jesus raises his friend Lazarus to life

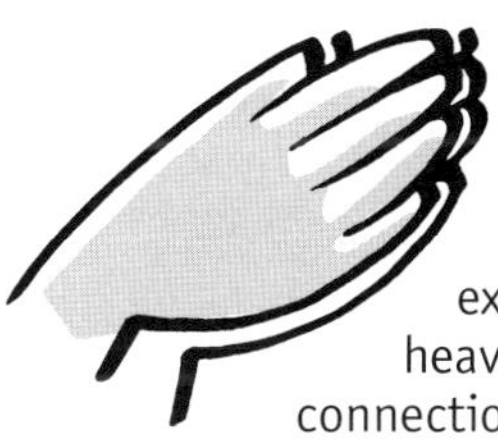

Prayer point

Praying with a child, individually or in a group, can be a very healing experience. Prayers addressed to a 'loving heavenly Father' seem to make more connections for a grieving child than 'Dear God'. Prayers should be real and from the heart. They could express our absolute trust in God's wisdom and love but equally they may express our horror or puzzlement at what has happened. Allow the children to pray their own short prayers if they want.

Helping a child when a significant relation has died

Children's lives revolve almost completely around their family and friendship groups. If someone close dies or is about to die, they have a very deep and real fear, not only for their own safety, but for the safety of the rest of their family and friends. They may...

- distance themselves from the person as they come close to dying
- avoid reference to the person who has died for fear of further upsetting other family members
- withdraw from friends or family
- be anxious at any separation from the rest of the family
- express anger towards God or a surviving parent for allowing the death to happen
- carry feelings of guilt
- become hostile and aggressive, alarming themselves as well as others.

These fears may suddenly re-emerge even years after they have apparently been resolved. Quiet reassurance and encouragement are probably all that a group leader can give, but these are very important.

Encourage attendance or at least the option to attend the final farewell ceremony or funeral. It is useful to give the grieving child their own 'sympathy' card and bunch of flowers. They can then choose whether they keep them themselves, put them on the coffin or give them to a surviving relative. It is very important that the child feels that there is still some part of their life over which they have some control.

'What happened to Grandma?'

It is important *not* to say 'Jesus wanted her more than we did' or 'She fell asleep'. These careless phrases may leave a child feeling that Jesus must be very selfish to take her away from us, or they may leave the child with a genuine fear of falling asleep at night. Talk simply about someone *dying* or that they are *dead* or that *death* occurred. You could explain that God loves her even more than we do and we have to trust him. She is at peace now.

'Has he gone for ever?'

Point out that our bodies are only part of us. After death a person can no longer experience hot or cold or the need to be hugged or held. He or she no longer feels pain or distress. Their body is like a set of clothes that has been discarded and left behind. It can either be turned to ashes in a special box called a coffin in a crematorium or be buried in a coffin in the ground at a cemetery. Sometimes a stone with a special message on it will mark the place and people can go there to be quiet and remember. For a Christian there is the firm belief that one day God will give us all new bodies – even better than these ones. And we will live with him for ever.

'When can we go to the park?'

With younger children be prepared to talk about changes in routine that might be causing them confusion. It is sometimes useful to get younger children to paraphrase what you have told them just to make sure that there are no real misconceptions.

Chat Box

'I don't like Mummy crying all the time.'

The slightly older child will need to be reassured that everyone has different reactions to death. It may not hit until the funeral, next Christmas or a birthday or anniversary. Give them permission to cry either by talking or by example, but say that *not* crying is all right too.

For Instance

I run a 'Happy-Sad' bereavement club for primary school children. More than half of the fifty members have experienced the death of a significant relation. In preparation, I had basic training from CRUSE, attended a few courses and talked to a lot of people. Essentially, however, I use basic listening skills, throw in a few ideas and then allow the children to take the lead. They are far more willing, in the right environment, to deal with 'taboo' issues in an up-front and direct way. I asked them recently what they found most useful about being allowed to talk about their grief. The following are some of their replies:

- 'You sometimes forget things so it helps you remember' *(Jo)*
- 'You can share your feelings' *(Kayla)*
- 'You can be nice to people who have had a sad happening' *(Daniel)*
- 'You get to talk about stuff and you don't have to keep it locked inside' *(Mia)*

Amy's story

Amy is nine years old. She comes from a Christian family. She used to have a little sister called Lisa but she can't remember much about her because she died when Amy was very small.

Amy's mum was called Linda. She was very pretty and lots of fun to be with. When Linda started getting ill, all the family prayed for God's love and peace in their home. Linda soon had to use a wheelchair as she could not walk any more. Amy had rides on the wheelchair. Linda was always full of joy and laughter.

Two years ago, Linda died. Amy went to the hospital to say goodbye. Amy was very sad but her friends cuddled her and helped her to talk about her mum. Linda had a beautiful Christian funeral. There were lots of tears and lots of thanks for her life. Amy's family have missed Linda badly but they still trust in their loving heavenly Father. Amy has sometimes felt very angry and confused but, with her dad's support, she is growing into a lovely young lady. She is now helping other children who have been bereaved.

Further help

CRUSE – bereavement groups all over the country (addresses of local groups are in phone books).

Reference books:

W Sydney Callaghan, *Good Grief,* Fount.

Ann Chadwick, *Living with Grief in School,* Family Reading Centre.

Wendy Duffy, *The Bereaved Child,* The National Society.

Atle Dyregrov, *Grief in Children,* JKP.

Janet Goodall, *Children and Grieving,* Scripture Union.

Books to use with a group of children:

Sarah Bowen, *Laura's Granny,* Scripture Union.

Judith Friedman, *Losing Uncle Tim,* Albert Whitman Prairie.

Marge Heegaard, *When Someone Has A Serious Illness,* Woodland Press.*

Marge Heegaard, *When Someone Very Special Dies,* Woodland Press.*

J Krementz, *How it Feels When a Parent Dies,* Gollanz.

Carolyn Nystrom, *What Happens When We Die?,* Scripture Union.

Ginny Perkins, *Remembering my Brother,* A & C Black.

Susan Varley, *Badger's Parting Gifts,* Collins Picture Lions.

** workbooks that can be obtained through St Christopher's Hospice, 51–59, Lawrie Park Road, London SE26 6DZ*

Section 28

TEACHING SESSION: Death

Psalm 23

Leaders' help

Psalm 23 describes God as a shepherd guiding and protecting his flock. The first few verses portray the shepherd's concern. He is personally interested in each of his sheep, making provision for them to drink, feed and rest in complete safety. Even in the most dark and difficult places, under the threat of death, he is there with them. His shepherd's staff is ready to direct and encourage.

In the last verses the picture changes. Now the psalmist is an honoured guest at a banquet. He is confident that he will receive his greatest desire – to live with God for ever.

Aim

To help the children to see that Jesus will always be with us even when someone dies and that we can trust him to understand our saddest feelings.

Way in

Talk with the children about people who have died: relatives, friends, people in the news or on films, even pets. Talk about how the children felt about these deaths; ask them what they remember about the funeral, and what they remember about the person or animal who has died. Use a storybook (perhaps one of the titles listed on page 44) to share some more ideas about death.

Tell it

Read out Psalm 23 from the *Good News Bible*.

Make a big picture together of a scene with some sheep. Start with a large piece of paper (e.g. lining or wallpaper). Draw a few lines on it to indicate some hilly countryside, and show where the green grassy areas, pools, paths and dark places will be. It does not need to be too artistic. Provide a variety of materials of different colours, e.g. colour magazines, paper, bits of fabric. Ask the children to work on different sections of the picture, cutting and sticking the material on the background. Finish by adding some blobs of cotton wool for sheep and the figure of a shepherd.

As the children work, ask them what they think a sheep needs if it's to be properly looked after. Explain that in Bible times, the shepherd would stay with his sheep all the time, leading them over the hills to find the best grass and water. He carried a big club to protect them from wild animals. Invite the children to ask any questions they have about the psalm.

When the picture is finished, look at it together and read the psalm again.

Apply it

Explain that some of the 'deepest darkness' we go through is when someone has died. God is with us in that situation. He is there to comfort us. He knows what it is to have a very close family member die. Ask the children to suggest ways in which God provides comfort for people when someone has died. Can we think about some helpful things that have happened to make life a little easier? What comfort or support have others in the group experienced? Can we think of other things that we could do to comfort someone else both individually and in the group?

If there are practical ideas which you can carry out, work out how you will do these.

Respond to God

Pray for people who are suffering the loss of someone at the moment. If a particular death has led to your doing a session on death, pray for everyone who is sad.

'Thank you Jesus for ____________________

You understand how each one of us is feeling at this moment.

Please comfort ____________________

and ____________________

who are missing them so much. Help them to know that you are close to them and love them. Thank you most of all for your special promise that one day we will all live together with you. Amen.'

Finish with some food as a reminder of the banquet that God has in store for us, and the life with him that we will have for ever.

Section 29

Moving on

Linda Stone

Change is a part of growing up. Whether it means physically growing, changing school or moving house, it is a regular experience for most. Children react in many different ways to change but they will all react in some way. It is unhelpful to grade change – some things might seem 'bigger' than other things (i.e. moving house into another town compared to changing maths set at school) but children react differently to different experiences and it is wrong to belittle any of their fears.

For children with only a few years of life experienced, a few months for things to settle will seem like a lifetime. The fear of change might bring about a change in behaviour.

Where a change affects the whole family, e.g. a house move, parents might be so occupied with tasks that they don't notice their child's fear. In this case a group leader may be able to offer the listening ear they need. Children need reassurance when facing change. A brief conversation with you may be what they need to help them through it.

Whatever the change, send a card to show the child that you are thinking of them and praying for them. If they are moving out of the area, continue to write or send a birthday or Christmas card. They may not write much back, but keep up the contact as long as it seems helpful.

Bible help

'Be strong and courageous. Do not be terrified; do not be discouraged, for the Lord your God will be with you wherever you go.'
Joshua 1:9

The people of Israel had taken forty years to get to their new home in the promised land. Now they stood on the brink of a huge change. But the big encouragement was that God was with them and would stay with them wherever they went and whatever happened. This verse can be a great encouragement to a child or adult facing change.

Prayer point

Agree to pray for the child at the critical time – as they arrive at the new school, leave their present home, meet their new teacher.

Further help

Jo Bailey, *Moving On...*, Scripture Union.

Mary Howard, *Little Ted Lost,* Scripture Union.

'Will I like my new school?'

'Will I make new friends?'

'Will anyone play with me?'

'Will I get lost?

Don't fob the child off with a simple 'It'll be fine.' Listen carefully to their specific worries. Be honest in saying that the new school will probably feel very strange to begin with but that it will become easier as they find their way around and get to know people. Encourage them to be bold about asking others to play with them.

'Where will the dog sleep in our new house?'

'But I like our old flat.'

'Will I have my own bedroom?'

The child may well be worried about details of a move which seem trivial. Encourage the child to ask their parents, or help by talking with the child and parent at the end of the session. Acknowledge the pain of leaving things behind, but encourage the child to see moving as an adventure; be really positive about new experiences, new places to discover and the possibility of choosing something new (curtains, perhaps) for their room.

Resources

Resources from CPAS

CPAS Code			
03690	It's Tough Being an Infant	Irene Brown	SU
03134	Working With Under 6s	Val Mullally	SU
92415	Caring for Children in Crèches and Toddler Groups	Ann Croft	CPAS
18006	The ART of 3-11s		CPAS
18003	Time for Children	George Lihou	CPAS
03576	Seen and Heard	Jackie Cray	CPAS
03684	Pastoral Care for Young People	Mark Vernon (Editor)	Oasis
03601	The Questions Children Ask	Penny Frank	CPAS

CPAS Sales, Athena Drive, Tachbrook Park, WARWICK, CV34 6NG
Tel: 01926 458400

CPAS Youth and Children's Division is available for consultation and training on all areas of youth and children's work. Please phone for more information.

Resources from Scripture Union

Margaret Barfield, *Tingling Tums,* Scripture Union, 1 85999 029 0.

Kathy Lee, *Deadly Emily,* Scripture Union, 1 85999 184 X.

Jan Godfrey, *Yellow Wellies,* Scripture Union, 1 85999 051 7.

Scripture Union books are available from your local Christian bookshop, or from SU Mail Order, PO Box 764, Oxford, OX4 5FJ (Tel: 01865 716880; Fax: 01865 715152).

SU Sales and Promotion, 207-209 Queensway, Bletchley, Milton Keynes, MK2 2EB (Tel: 01908 856000; Fax: 01908 856111).

Other general resources

Joan King (ed.), *Family and All That Stuff,* NCEC.

Eugene Peterson, *Five Smooth Stones for Pastoral Care,* Gracewing.

William Kay and Paul Weaver, *Pastoral Care and Counselling: a manual,* Paternoster.

Resource agencies

Agencies that help in many areas of pastoral care

ChildLine (Tel: 0800 1111) – a free 24-hour helpline for children to ring. They also produce helpful leaflets on bullying and abuse.

NSPCC, 42 Curtain Road, LONDON, EC2A 3NH (Tel: 0800 800 500) – provides useful leaflets on abuse and its prevention, listening to children, and issues of parenting.

Kidscape, 152 Buckingham Palace Road, LONDON, SW1W 9TR (Tel: 0171 730 3300) – a charity campaigning for children's safety.

Agencies that help in specific areas of pastoral care

Church Action on Disability, 50 Scrutton Street, LONDON, EC2A 4PH (Tel: 0171 452 2085), and RADAR, 12 City Forum, 250 City Road, LONDON, EC1V 8AF (Tel: 0171 250 3222) – offer help, support and action on disability issues.

Dyslexia Association, 98 London Road, READING, RG1 5AU (Tel: 0118 966 8271).

Anti Bullying Campaign, 10 Borough High Street, LONDON, SE1 9QQ (Tel: 0171 378 1446).

The Churches Child Protection Advisory Service (part of PCCA Christian Child Care) PCCA, PO Box 133, SWANLEY, Kent, BR8 7UQ (Tel: 01322 667207/660011) – advises and supports churches on issues of child abuse and child protection, providing workpacks and training materials. It also offers advice and support on issues of fostering and adoption.

Family Mediators Association (FMA), 1 Wyvil Court, Wyvil Road, LONDON, SW8 2TG (E-mail: info@familymediators.co.uk) – provides information about helping children experiencing divorce and new family situations.

National Stepfamily Association UK, 3rd Floor Chapel House, 18 Hatton Place, LONDON, EC1N 8RU (Tel: 0171 209 2460).

Gingerbread, 1617 Clerkenwell Close, LONDON, EC1R 0AA (Tel: 0171 336 8183; E-mail: general_enquiry@gingerbread.org.uk) – lone parents' association.

CRUSE – bereavement groups all over the country. GPs often need to give a referral for counselling.

Resources for specific issues

For details of other publications relating to specific areas of pastoral care, please see the relevant sections in this book.

THE YOUTH AND CHILDREN DIVISION OF CPAS

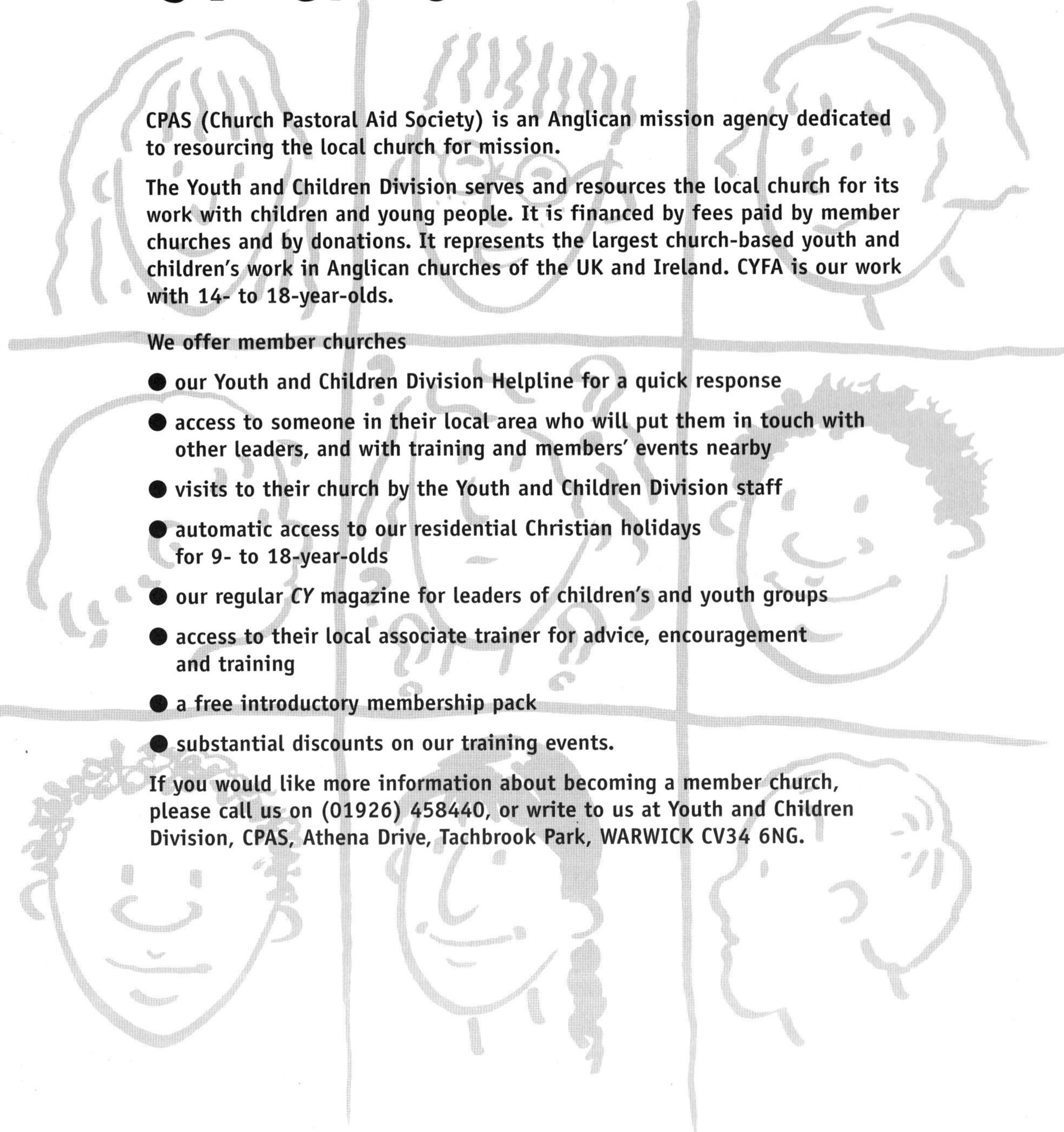

CPAS (Church Pastoral Aid Society) is an Anglican mission agency dedicated to resourcing the local church for mission.

The Youth and Children Division serves and resources the local church for its work with children and young people. It is financed by fees paid by member churches and by donations. It represents the largest church-based youth and children's work in Anglican churches of the UK and Ireland. CYFA is our work with 14- to 18-year-olds.

We offer member churches

- our Youth and Children Division Helpline for a quick response
- access to someone in their local area who will put them in touch with other leaders, and with training and members' events nearby
- visits to their church by the Youth and Children Division staff
- automatic access to our residential Christian holidays for 9- to 18-year-olds
- our regular *CY* magazine for leaders of children's and youth groups
- access to their local associate trainer for advice, encouragement and training
- a free introductory membership pack
- substantial discounts on our training events.

If you would like more information about becoming a member church, please call us on (01926) 458440, or write to us at Youth and Children Division, CPAS, Athena Drive, Tachbrook Park, WARWICK CV34 6NG.